GIOVANNA MAGI

ALL MILAN

205 color photographs
city map

BET
BONECHI EDIZIONI «IL TURISMO» - FIRENZE

© Copyright 1998 by Bonechi Edizioni "Il Turismo" S.r.l
Via dei Rustici, 5 -50122 Firenze
Tel. +39 (55) 239.82.24/25 - Fax +39 (55) 21.63.66
http://www.bonechi.com
e-mail: barbara@bonechi.com / bbonechi@dada.it
Printed in Italy

Photographs: Bonechi Archives and Edizioni Scrocchi, Milan.
Aerial photos by: I-Buga, Milan (p. 3 - Aut. S.M.A. 256/82; p. 17 - Aut.
S.M.A.781/83) and Pubbli Aer Foto, Milan (p. 39 - Aut. S.M.A. 401/69;
p. 111 - Aut. S.M.A. 412/72; p. 114 - Aut. S.M.A. 401/69)
Lay-out: Piero Bonechi
Editing: Barbara Bonechi
Typesetting: Leadercomp, Florence
Photolithography: La Fotolitografia, Florence
Printing: BO.BA.DO.MA., Florence
ISBN 88-7204-011-6

er Milan was made capital of the XI Transpadane region. The city's military, political, and economic importance grew to such an extent that Milan, under Diocletian's decree, as part of the new order of the empire became the seat of the Augustian realm of the West. Even after it lost its standing as seat of the empire, Milan retained its civil and military importance – so much so that in 313 Constantine issued the famous edict of Milan by which the Christian religion was officially recognized throughout the Roman Empire in the city. The year 370 marked the arrival of a new bishop, St. Ambrose, in Milan. His great wisdom, equilibrium, and unshaking faith played an important role in placating the religious controversies raging at the time and this led to a highly profitable collaboration with the emperor Theodosius. The death of these two great men, the threat of an invasion by the Visgoths led by Alaricus, plus the transfer of the capital of the Roman Empire to a safer city, Ravenna, were all factors in slowing Milan's development. By 409 the city came under the rule of the Ostrogoths. It must be said for their leader Theodoric, however, that he did make an attempt to have his barbarians get along with the local population. In 535 the war that the Emperor of the East, Justinian allied with the Italian Christians, waged against the Goths brought about the city's downfall. All but abandoned and defenseless, Milan was put to siege for over a year. Finally forced to surrender at the point of starvation, the city was sacked and destroyed and the population slaughtered. Reconstruction had just gotten under way, when the Longobards – whose chief Alboinus decided to settle in nearby Pavia – came along, soon to be followed by Charlemagne's Franks in 774. Conquest by the Franks, who placed great stress on religious matters, meant that the figure of the archbishop – whose authority arrived where civil and military power could not – took on increasing importance in the city. Following Charlemagne's death, the long, drawnout squabbling of his successors led to the downfall of Pavia and the destruction of Charlemagne's royal palace. Pavia's downfall was the starting point for Milan's rebirth and recovery, from the time of Archbishop Aribertus d'Intimianus, leader by virtue of his exceptional political, military, and moral stature. Nevertheless, the growing awareness of the newborn lower class, the cives, brought about social upheaval and unrest, soon intensified by the ferment stemming from discord over the Papal investiture. In order to re-affirm the city's autonomy once and for all, the Archbishop of Milan, in agreement with the local aristocrats, took over the administration of everything that had previously belonged to the emperor. And so the Free City State (Comune) was born. As part of the new atmosphere the economy of the town developed hand in hand with that of the countryside. Of course, economic expansion involved territorial expansion and soon Como, Lodi, Pavia, Piacenza, and Tortona succumbed to the Milanese. Then in 1158 Frederick I Barbarossa (Redbeard) put a brusque halt to these conquests when he occupied the city. Although in the following years the city attempted to rid itself of the invaders time and time again, Frederick succeeded in asserting his authority, first by beseiging Milan for seven months and then by completely destroying it in 1162. Milan soon rose from the ashes and this time, allied with the other Lombard City States she had previously attempted to conquer, rebelled against the emperor's authority. The outcome was the formation of the famous Lombard League which, according to tradition, was consecrated at Pontida in April 1167. The much augured League of the City States emerged victorious from the Battle of Legnano (May 29, 1176) which led to Barbarossa's recognition of the autonomy of the Free City States and the drawing up of the peace treaty of Costanza. But the union of the Lombard Free City States did not last very long, since as soon as the threat posed by Barbarossa vanished, internal conflicts broke out among the cities united in the confederations known as the Milan and Cremona Leagues. At the same time that events in the empire led to deep changes in the political make-up of the cities and thus a change from the Free City State Stage to that of the Podestà (governorship), in Milan a greater popular cohesiveness brought about the change from Free City State to the Signoria (titled rulers). The first to seize power was the Della Torre family later supplanted by the famous Viscontis. Under their rule, Milan became the capital of a powerful, tightly organized state which was able to intervene in the most important Italian affairs and even influence them. The Visconti lords ruled Milan for 130 years, many of which were characterized by events that were always extremely intricate and often extremely obscure. Under the domination of Ludovico il Moro, Milan reached an extraordinary degree of splendor. Leonardo da Vinci was received by the court (and remained in Milan for 18 years till 1499) while at the same time the city was being embellished by the works of Bramante and growing by leaps and bounds. Ludovico, however, made the mistake of toppling the precarious equilibrium among the Italian states, thereby favoring the intervention of the French King, Charles VIII. Everything turned against him when the new king of France Louis XII proclaimed himself legitimate heir to the Duchy of Milan by virtue of his relationship to the Viscontis. After Ludovico's defeat, the French domination of Milan did not last a long time, but the city's power had been seriously undermined by the Pope on one side and the new Swiss threat on the other. Italy had become the battlefield of the great European powers and the Duchy of Milan was the first to suffer the consequences. Contended by both France and Spain, after a series of ups and downs, it fell into the hands of the Spanish. This proved to be the longest domination that Milan would ever experience: it lasted from 1535 to 1713, a time of mortification, humiliation, and disappointments but also of hope which never flickered out. Yet, despite the two plague epidemics of 1576 and 1629, the economy of the city, even though it failed to achieve great development, never did die out altogether. During these dark years, Milan was illuminated by two great figures, first St. Carlo Borromeo and then Federico Borromeo. The war of the Spanish Succession also brought a new master to take control of the city: Austria. Milan also took an active part in the Enlightenment which had spread throughout all of 18th century Europe. Cesare Beccaria, Giuseppe Parini, and Pietro Verri are examples of well-known Milanese intellectuals of the period. Abandoned by Austria, Milan came under still another foreign yoke. Napoleon Bonaparte made his entrance into the city on May 15, 1796 and on July 9 the city was proclaimed capital of the Cisalpine Republic. Though subjected to France, it nevertheless managed to preserve

The Battle of Legnano, by Amos Cassioli (Gallery of Modern Art, Florence).

its own culture and way of life. Just three years later the Austrians again took over the city. With an iron heel they suppressed all of the civil liberties and democratic institutions created by the French emperor. But not for long. Napoleon, victorious at Marengo, reconstructed the Cisalpine Republic in Milan, the only symbol of a national state in the whole group of bickering Italian states. Milan thus became a beacon for the pro-unity patriots whose thirst for liberty was intensified by the intolerance of the regimes of the day. Ugo Foscolo, the poet, and Vincenzo Cuoco, the writer, are two well-known examples. On May 26, 1805 Napoleon crowned himself with the iron crown in Milan and a new period of splendor dawned on the city under the rule of viceroy Eugène Beauharnais. Then the defeat of Napoleon at Leipzig and his definitive downfall brought Milan back under Austria's iron heel. Every means was employed in an effort to save the Reign of Italy and with it any form of free rule, but the hopes of the Milanese were soon dashed, for on June 12, 1814 Lombardy was annexed to the Austrian Empire. The return of the Austrians, welcomed by the conservative bourgeoisie, was of course a bane to the patriots, from then on more numerous and better organized than ever, despite the terrible punishments inflicted if they were captured. From 1815 to 1848 intellectual growth and economic development proceeded hand in hand. Literary movements sprang up and new journals and magazines were founded. But this was also the period of great arrests and great trials, the period in which the famous revolt of 1848 was brewing. The climax was reached between March 19 and 23, 1848 – the famous "Cinque

Giornate" (5 Days) of Milan. The Milanese arose against their oppressor during five days of bitter fighting and Radetzky, the Austrian General, was forced to abandon the city. The temporary government opted for annexation to the Kingdom of Sardinia, but Carlo Alberto was soundly beaten by Austria and thus the Austrians were once more back in the city. Ten more years of foreign domination and another war broke out. On June 8, 185 the king of Italy, Victor Emanuel II, and the king of France, Napoleon III, triumphantly entered Milan. Milan thus became part of the newborn Italian state, naturally with all due importance and prestige. Throughout the first century of Italian history – now that Italy was at long last a united nation – Milan's contribution to cultural life was outstanding. The city offered fertile terrain for the flowering of literary, philosophical, and political movements. Not even the obscure period of Fascism which followed on the heels of World War I was able to ruin Milan's heritage. Indeed the city became one of the most active centers of anti-Mussolini propaganda and of the Resistance itself. World War II brought new mourning and fresh destruction caused by the terrible air bombardments of 1943. The same year, on September 8 Milan was occupied by the Germans, but the Milanese triumphantly beat them back during the insurrection of April 25, 1945. As soon as the war scars started to heal the Milanese made even more grandiose that which the war had destroyed or caused to be left unfinished. Always at the avantguard culturally, at the forefront of Italian economy and industry, Milan more than ever had a starring role in the drama of Italian life.

View of Piazza del Duomo; on the following pages: the Cathedral.

PIAZZA DEL DUOMO

Milan's population more than doubled in the postwar years which meant that the city bulged out way beyond the original boundaries of old Milan – the canals known as the Navigli – and today factories and housing projects continue to engulf what was once countryside. But the people residing in the remote outskirts have a hard time feeling they are actually living in Milan, for the throbbing heart of Milan is Piazza del Duomo, right in the midst of the downtown section. The whole city seems to evolve around the square: people are everywhere, either on their way to the office or factory, a shopping or theater date, or else slowly strolling around and window-shopping the fashionable stores under the arcade. The huge rectangular square was renovated in the 19th century by Giuseppe Mengoni who restored all the surrounding buildings to harmonize with the Cathedral, which makes an ideal background setting. The two long sides are actually arcaded buildings, the North Building and the South Building, the former pierced by the triumphal arch of the Vittorio Emanuele Arcade and the latter followed by two minor arcaded buildings of 1939 known as the "propilei". In the center of the square is

Ercole Rosa's 1896 equestrian monument to Vittorio Emanuele II. The Italian king is portrayed as he incites his soldiers on to victory in the Battle of St. Martin. The figure of the king as he reins in his horse and turns to address his men is in keeping with the extremely naturalistic treatment of the whole. Along the base is a relief depicting the Piedmont and French troops entering Milan and on either side is a marble lion. But the most fascinating sights are below and not on Cathedral Square! Important archeological finds were unearthed during a dig in 1942 and the experts soon came to the conclusion that the ruins they had discovered were actually the remains of the basilica of St. Tecla – originally built in the 4th century and then later rebuilt and rebuilt throughout the centuries until the building was finally torn down in the 15th century. Other remains brought to light behind St. Tecla come from the octagonal-shaped Baptistery of St. John of the Font, it too dating back to the 4th century, and lastly, on the same site as the Cathedral, the basilica of St. Maria Maggiore, which gradually disappeared to make way for the giant cathedral.

THE BUILDING
OF THE CATHEDRAL

Few churches in Italy underwent such a slow, complex building process as Milan's cathedral. In addition, putting up such a gigantic monument involved not only Lombardy but actually all of Italy. It was, in fact, through the cathedral that the High Gothic style from beyond the Alps made its way down to Milan and henceforth influenced the whole country. Progress was painstakingly slow: work actually went on throughout five centuries, although the original Gothic style was never abandoned. The cathedral, dedicated to Mary, was actually begun in 1387 over the site of the 9th century basilica of St. Maria Maggiore. Built on the express wish of Archbishop Antonio da Saluzzo, the initiative found favor with Gian Galeazzo Visconti (then ruler of the city) and the whole Milanese population. For that year the chief engineer was Simone da Orsegnigo who was aided by several Campionese (Swiss) masons. Nevertheless, the overall design of the cathedral was undoubtedly conceived by a sole mastermind, an artist definitely from beyond the Alps since, despite the fact that numerous architects had a hand in it, the cathedral never lost its amazing cohesiveness – a characteristic so typical of the work of Northern masters. It must be said, however, that the Gothic schemes in the hands of the Italian architects lost much of their Northern flavor and acquired a more typically Italian feeling. Simone da Orsenigo was surrounded by a crew of great stonemasons: Marco "de Frixono" of Campione, Matteo da Campione, and the greatest of all, Giovannino de' Grassi. In 1389 da Orsenigo was dismissed and Nicola di Bonaventura was summoned from Paris. Nicola designed the huge pierced windows of the apse after his arrival in Milan on May 7, 1389, but he too was dismissed (on July 31, 1390). Italian and foreign master craftsmen followed one another; among them we may cite the Germans Johann from Freiburg, Heinrich Parler from Gmünden, Ulrich from Füssingen, Hans von Fernach, and the Italians Bernardo da Venezia, Gabriele Stornaloco, Marco da Carona, Giovannino de' Grassi and Giacomo da Campione. The latter two worked permanently in the cathedral workshop from 1392 on and left their imprint in the use of the so-called "flowery Gothic" style known for its flamboyant decorative patterns. After the death of the great master de' Grassi, the Parisan Jean Mignot, sharply critical of what had been previously done, was put in charge, but opposed by Bernardo da Venezia and Bertolino da Novara, he was soon fired, and from then on the building of the Cathedral of Milan was supervised exclusively by Italian masters. In 1400 Filippino degli Ugoni became supervisor of the project; the capitals, vaulting, and terraces are of his design. Work went on at such a fast pace that by 1418 the main altar could be consecrated by Pope Martin V. When Francesco Sforza came to power in the mid 15th century, art in Milan was absorbing French and Tuscan influences. 15th century Milanese architecture and thus also that of the cathedral was strongly influenced by three generations of the Solari family: Giovanni Solari, his son Guinforte, and Guinforte's son Pier Antonio. Guinforte's son-in-law, the

The Cathedral's façade.

great Giovanni Antonio Amadeo, won the competition called in 1490 for the building of the drum. Despite the new Renaissance turn art had taken, Amadeo was a strenuous defender of the structure's Gothic unity. He completed the drum by 1500. Ten years later the first of the four adjacent spires was put up it too in the Gothic style. Meanwhile the great surge of "flowery Gothic" was gradually losing momentum, beaten by the new more plastic treatment of form advocated by Filarete, Luca Francelli, Francesco di Giorgi, and Leonardo, summoned from all over Italy to give fresh advice and up-to-date opinions on how the cathedral should be built. After a brief German intervention, a master called by Gian Galeazzo Sforza from Strasburg in 1482, Pellegri Pellegrini, also known as Tibaldi, the favorite archite of Archbishop Carlo Borromeo, was named masterm son. Pellegrini immediately threw himself into the j and designed the patterns for the flooring and cho stalls. In 1572 Borromeo reconsecrated the cathedral. 1585, when Pellegrini left for Spain, he got Marti Bassi and then later Lelio Buzzi, who had earli designed the Ambrosian Library, to take over. When th other great Borromeo, Federico, was archbishop, Fab Mangoni was put in charge of the cathedral buildin followed by Richini and the Quadrios, but the 18 century was ushered in and it was still incomplete. T

The absidal portion of the Cathedral.

t spire was erected between 1765 and 1769 and the
...de, based on Pellegrini's idea, was put up between
... and 1813. Work went on right through the 19th
...ury, during which time the spires and the towers
... stairways inside were completed. The whole com-
... construction, however, was badly in need of restora-
... the first campaign was undertaken in 1935 and the
...nd – even more complicated and painful – after the
...bardments of 1943. During the latter restoration
...ect, the flooring was restored and the statues and
...rative elements which had suffered the greatest war
...age were replaced. Finally, on December 8, 1966, the
...churchyard was dedicated.

Apse – The apse, i.e. rear section, is the most genuinely Gothic
part of the whole cathedral. The imposing polygonal apses are
emphasized by enormous buttresses spanning three huge
windows designed by Filippino degli Organi. The thin ribs
creating lovely patterns all over the windows culminate in a
charming rose motif. This special embroidery with marble
thread, here carried to the utmost of skill, attains an unusual
degree of complexity and fantasy. The rhythmic pattern
created by the ribs and buttresses continues along the sides of
the building. From a breathtaking aerial view we can better
observe the daring structure of the Cathedral whose conception
is based on the bearing strength of the piers and buttresses.
Above these architectural members is a fairytale decorative
world of pinnacles, spires, and statues.

The Cathedral: doors and buttresses; below: the main door and one of the panels.

Center doorway – The façade of the cathedral has fiv[e]
Baroque doorways with double buttresses by the centr[al]
doorway and on the outside and single buttresses on the insid[e]
The pilasters rest on heavy bases, each of which bears a 17th c[entury]
18th century relief, above which are talamons (human for[m]
architectural members) of the same period. The middle doo[r]
was executed by Castelli and Bono in 1635. The Creation [of]
Eve depicted in the huge bas-relief of Carrara marble over th[e]
door was executed by Gaspare Vismara after a design b[y]
Giovan Battista Crespi known as Cerano. The parastas whic[h]
frame the doorway with their luxuriant flower, fruit, an[d]
animal motifs were designed by the Baroque artist Richini. Th[e]
bronze door on the inside however is a modern work execute[d]
by Ludovico Pogliaghi between 1894 and 1908. The arti[st]
imitated the flowery Gothic style in his reliefs depicting scene[s]
from the life of the Virgin.

The central nave; right: the door to the southern sacristy, by Hans von Fernach, ca. 1393.

Interior – Entering the church, we are struck more by a feeling of stylistic consistency than by the huge size of the building itself. It is worth one's while to take a good look at the interior of this church which is the biggest Gothic church and second biggest church (after St. Peter's in Rome) in the world. It measures 514 feet long by 302 feet wide and soars 585 feet into the air. The nave is marked by 52 stately compound piers which rise up to meet the arches, pointed as befits the Gothic style. This upward movement of the piers is interrupted by the unusual capitals which are actually separate little tabernacles between the piers and the arch itself. The dome, 221 feet above our heads, rises on four pointed arches and is quite awe inspiring from both technical and esthetic standpoints. But we must not fail to mention the wealth of art works around us. For example, the stunning doorway which leads to the southside sacristy should not be overlooked. Dated circa 1393, it was executed by Hans von Fernach, one of the many German masters who worked alongside Italian colleagues during the long genesis of the cathedral. The numerous carved sculptures were once colored. In the lintel frieze the Wise and Foolish

The Cathedral crypt; left: the bronze Trivulzio candelabrum attributed to the French goldsmith, Nicolas de Verdun, early 13th century.

Virgins are represented, while the Deposition of Christ and th[e] Virgin amidst the pious are depicted on the inner lunette an[d] six scenes from the life of Christ are portrayed under th[e] archway.

Miscellaneous – Among the various works worthy of mentio[n] in the Cathedral are the monument to Gian Giacomo Medi[ci] considered the masterpiece of Leone Leoni (right aisle of th[e] right transept). Executed between 1560 and 1563, it wa[s] erected in honor of Pope Pius IV's brother who died in 155[5.] Typically 16th century in style, e.g. bronze bas-relief emergin[g] from a marble background, the statue in the middle depict[s] Gian Giacomo clad in Roman armour, while personifications [of]

PIVS·IIII·PONT·MAX·FRA·B·FIERI·I

Funerary monument to Gian Giacomo Medici by Leone
Leoni, 16th century; right: St. Bartholomew Flayed, by
Marco d'Agrate, 1562.

ar and Peace stand on the left and right respectively. The
ulptor has purposely concealed the slightly bent left leg of the
ope's brother under a cloak to hide the fact that he was a
ipple. Marco d'Agrate's Flaying of St. Bartholomew of 1562
such an amazingly accurate rendition of human anatomy that
e sculptor, in praise of his own great skill, was moved to
rve an inscription on the base which reads: This is by Marco
'Agrate and not by Praxiteles. Last but not least is the 16
ot tall, 7 branched Trivulzio Candelabrum donated by Giovan-
Trivulzio to the church on April 8, 1562. The Gothic bronze
asterpiece has been attributed to the French goldsmith
icolas de Verdun and dated early 1200's.

Three magnificent stained glass windows of the Cathedral; opposite page: **aerial view of the Cathedral.**

Stained glass windows – The photo above shows stained glass windows depicting from the left: the 2nd with scenes from the Old Testament, executed in different periods by different artists, among whom we may cite Nicolò da Varallo (1460), the 14th portraying scenes of the life of St. Catherine of Alexandria by Corrado de Mochis (1556) after a design by Biagio and Giuseppe Arcimboldi, and the 4th with scenes from the Old Testament. The latter was executed by German and Italian masters in the 16th century and Stefano and Antonio Pandino in 1475 and later restored by Bertini. The 2nd and 4th windows are located in the right aisles, the 14th is over the side entrance of the church.

Details of the terraces, lantern and pinnacles; the gilded copper statue of the Virgin, known as «La Madonnina» stands atop the highest pinnacle; it was sculpted by Giuseppe Bini, to a model by Giuseppe Perego, 1774 (photo on extreme right, opposite page).

Dome and terraces – When, during the first half of the 19 century the cathedral façade had finally been completed, it w decided to decorate the roof with a profusion of spire pinnacles, and statuary in keeping with the overall Gothic styl This crowning touch, a fitting conclusion to the centuries lo project and perhaps the most distinctive characteristic of th whole building, came to life under the skilled supervision Pestagalli. On reaching the terrace (there is a lift for th fainthearted) we have before us the lovely structure of th dome which looks like intricate stone embroidery. Designed Giovanni Antonio Amadeo in 1490 it was actually built in th 16th century at the same time as the tower facing northea Upon the tallest spire of all is the thirteen foot high gild copper statue of the Virgin known as the Madonnina which h become a symbol of the city of Milan. It was cast in 1774 by th goldsmith Bini.

Equestrian monument to Vittorio Emanuele II, by Ercole Rosa, in Piazza del Duomo.

VITTORIO EMANUELE ARCADE

The Galleria, in contrast to the delicate lacy effect of the Cathedral, dominates the square with its weighty bulk and great triumphal archway cut into the long, northern facade. Built between 1865 and 1877, it was designed by Giuseppe Mengoni who, just before the actual building was completed, fell from the scaffolding and plunged to his death. The cross-shaped structure is surmounted by an extraordinary colored glass and iron dome. The modern technical skill and originality of the Milan Galleria have nothing to fear from a comparison with similar structures put up in London and Paris about the same time. Today this glassed-in street is a center for both cultural and mundane activities with its well-stocked book and record shops, giant cafés, and famous eating spots.

Right: **the interior of the Vittorio Emanuele Arcade**;
below: **the front of the gallery.**

The Royal Palace by Giuseppe Piermarini.

PALAZZO REALE

The Royal Palace, known as Old Town Hall, was the Milan city hall starting from 1138, although its present appearance is due to a transformation by Piermarini during the 18th century in the Neo-Classical style. When the Visconti family took up residence here in 1310 it became a sumptuous aristocratic palace, seat of the Visconti's Ducal Court. Modifications were made on account of the cathedral going up next to it and as result of the transformations commissioned by its various owners, such as the Sforzas, the Spanish governor, and Archduke Ferdinand of Austria. Its superb interior with all the statues, frescoes, floors, and plasterworks was completely devastated by the 1943 bombardments. Since 1965 the Palace belongs to the city, and is now home to the Museum of Contemporary Art, while the left wing has long housed the Cathedral Museum.

CATHEDRAL MUSEUM

Opened in 1953 and recently enlarged, the Cathedral Museum occupies the left wing of the Palazzo Reale. All the works on display – drawings, paintings, plaster casts, models, and sculpture – are related to the building of the Cathedral. In fact, over the centuries, it was inevitable that a collection of pieces from different periods and styles should grow up – just like living pages torn from the Cathedral's history book. Room 12, or Sala delle Origini contains a fine statue of Gian Galeazzo Visconti. Executed by Giorgio Solari in 1404, it originally stood atop the Carelli pinnacle – from which it toppled during the 1943 bombardment. Another noteworthy work is the head of the Savior. The realistic rendering proves its Northern origin; probable dating is early 15th century. The wooden model of the cathedral, made by Bernardo Zenale da Treviglio in 1520, should not be overlooked.

Cathedral Museum - Interior of a room.

Cathedral Museum - Head of the Redeemer, 14th century work in copper and gold; right: statue of Gian Galeazzo Visconti, by Giorgio Solari, 1404.

nor should the drawings of the façade – ranging from Pellegrini's 16th century rendition to Buzzi's more recent one.

The lovely bell tower of San Gottardo in Corte.

SAN GOTTARDO IN CORTE

Only the lovely apse and the even lovelier belltower are left of the church Pecorari was commissioned to build by Azzone Visconti between 1330 and 1336 for the court of the Visconti lords. The tower is quite unusual. It starts out square-shaped, then becomes an octagon, and is topped with a cone cap. The Neo-Classical interior contains a fragment of a Crucifixion scene frescoed by an unknown follower of the Florentine master Giotto in c 1350, as well as other frescoes commissioned by the Visconti family from Tuscan masters whose style o painting already foreshadowed the new Renaissanc manner – the seeds of which were planted during th early 14th century by the great Giotto himself in farof Tuscany.

The exterior of La Scala; right: Pietro Magni's monument to Leonardo da Vinci stands at the middle of Piazza della Scala.

PIAZZA DELLA SCALA

Crossing the Vittorio Emanuele Arcade from south to north, we come out in the famous Piazza della Scala. On the far side of the square we see La Scala Theater and opposite us is Palazzo Marino, today Milan's City Hall. The monument in the center of the square portrays Leonardo da Vinci surrounded by his pupils. Galeazzo Alessi was commissioned by the 16th century Genovese merchant Tommaso Marino – a real tycoon in his day – to design the palace. One of its more striking features is the vast inner courtyard with an unusual decorative scheme of human and animal head sculptures surrounded by carved garlands and geometric patterns.

Another view of La Scala.

LA SCALA THEATER

Italy's best-known theater La Scala is where world famous composers, singers, and orchestra conductors make their debuts. It is located alongside the church of St. Maria della Scala, built by Bernabò Visconti's wife, Regina della Scala, in 1381. By the time La Scala was officially inaugurated on August 3, 1778 with Antonio Salieri's "Europa Riconosciuta", Milan already possessed a theater of its own: Giandomenico Barbieri's, built in 1717, was located in a wing of the present day Royal Palace. Perhaps opera was so slow to catch on in Milan, compared to other Italian and European cities, on account of the violent attacks on light comedy and

theater in general made by Carlo Borromeo towards t[?] end of the 16th century. Then too war, famine, plagu[?] and poverty had kept the Milanese from thinking abo[?] theatrical amusements for hundreds of years. Fina[?] ly,after having to make do with plain rooms and temp[?] rary theaters. the emperor commissioned Barbieri to [?] out a wing of his palace as a theater. From then o[?] opera thrived in Milan, but unfortunately, during t[?] night of the Carnival festivities of 1776, the theat[?] caught fire and nothing but ashes was left of its Baroq[?] stuccoed auditorium. By then, however, theater ha[?] taken hold in Milan and two months later plans we[?]

The interior of La Scala.

eing drawn up for a bigger and better building, even
ore beautiful than Barbieri's. Though the Archduke
erdinand approved the design, it was the Austrian
mpress Maria Theresa who actually financed the con-
ruction of the new theater which was miraculously
ompleted fifteen months later. That the architect,
iuseppe Piermarini, was a passionate advocate of the
eo-Classical school is clearly reflected in the façade of

the building: a jutting structure with the three lower
arcades, railing, and windows separated by double columns. The interior stands out for its uncluttered ele-
gance-especially if you compare it to the typical over-
stuccoed theater in vogue in the 18th century. Here the
simple effect is achieved by four rows of boxes (two
galleries were later added) and a stage set off by four
huges gold and white Corinthian columns.

The Theater Museum - La Scala Theater, oil painting by Angelo Inganni, 1852.

THEATER MUSEUM

The museum, founded at the turn of the century, actually houses three collections: the Giulio Sambon Collection acquired in Paris, the Verdi Collection, and the Theater Collection. Set up according to the newest museum criteria, the collections are an invaluable document relating not just to theater in Milan, but also to the development of theater in Italy and the worldover, from its birth up to our day. Step by step we can trace the history of drama from the Greek statues of Tanagra through Italian vases with portrayals of theatrical scenes, from the masks of Ancient Rome to the reliefs carved on the sarcophagi of Greek actors. The first

rooms are filled with portraits of the greats from th world of the renowned Commedia dell'Arte, such ; Giuseppe Biancolelli, known as Dominique, comic acte in Louis XIV's court and Scaramuzza and Crispin, bot celebrated 17th century comedians. Finally, there ai portraits of famous opera singers such as Giuditta Past. the great soprano form Lombardy for whom Vincenz Bellini wrote Norma and La Sonnambula (the bust wa sculpted by Comolli), Isabella Angela Colbran, singer an first wife of Gioacchino Rossini, and Maria Felicit Malibran, another great Bellini specialist. How can on fail to be awed within the walls of the one and only L

The Theater Museum - Above, from the left: **portrait of Giuseppe Verdi; portrait of Arturo Toscanini;** right: **portrait of Giacomo Puccini.**

cala, Italy's greatest opera house? Here Bellini, after aving gloried in two enormous successes, Pirata and La onnambula, was greeted with catcalls when Norma iserably flopped on December 26, 1831. Here on April 5, 1926 Giacomo Puccini's Turandot was premiered osthumously under the direction of Arturo Toscanini, ho after laying down his baton, turned to the emotion-led crowd and said, "Maestro Giacomo Puccini stops re". Here, opera lovers from Milan and all over Italy, itnessed the miracles of Verdi's genius when the great mposer, at the twilight of his career, held the audience ellbound with his Othello sung by Tamagno.

CASA DEGLI OMENONI

This 16th century palazzo (fittingly dubbed House of the Giants – Omenoni – by the Milanese) on the street of the same name, was originally the home and workshop of the Tuscan sculptor, Leone Leoni. Court sculptor to Charles V and Philip II of Spain and friend of Vasari, the Tuscan artist-biographer and Pietro Aretino, the Tuscan writer, Leoni built up one of the first Milanese art collections – among his "finds" was Leonardo's Atlantic Codex. Rather an odd fellow, he designed the sober façade of his house with eight colossal telamon figures flanking the windows and doorway. Sculpted by Antonio Abbondio, the figures create a genuinely striking and unforgettable effect.

Casa degli Omenoni, detail of the façade; below: apse of the church of San Fedele.

SAN FEDELE

St. Carlo Borromeo commissioned his favorite architect Pellegrini to design this church for the Jesuit order. Pellegrini's façade reflects the Baroque concept of inspiring religious architecture. Decorative elements such as cornices and columns enhance the splendor of the solid church structure, although the left side with its double row of columns is much plainer and less agitated in comparison. The magnificent interior has not been broken up by aisles, but divided into two sections by arches originating from pilasters against the walls.

PIAZZA MERCANTI

Miracously a corner of old Milan is still preserved intact here – it is hard to believe that traffic and skyscrapers are just a step away! Originally square shaped, it had six gates, one for each of the neighborhoods of the 13th

Piazza Mercanti.

ntury city. In the center stood the Palazzo della
agione, or New Town Hall, commissioned from 1228 to
33 by Oldrado di Tresseno, the first Milanese mayor,
rtrayed on horseback in a high relief above the
ace's fourth pillar; stylistically this work (1233) bears
e influence of the famous 12th century sculptor from
odena, Antelami. Below is a five verse Latin in-
ription exalting the mayor's major merits, i.e. one,
mmissioning this palace and two, burning heretics at
e stake. The extremely plain building has three rows of
cades supported by square pillars and a brickwork
per floor with triple windows. The charming Loggia
gli Osii commissioned by Matteo Visconti da Scoto of
n Gimignano in 1316, sharply contrasts with the
arkness of the palace. Although it was unfortunately

disfigured in the 17th and 18th centuries, we can still get
an idea of what it must have been like by the 1904
restoration which attempted to bring it back to its
original form. Built of black and white marble, it is
composed of two superimposed loggias with divided
windows along the top floor. Upon the upper loggia are
coats of arms of the various districts and of the Visconti
family and in the middle is the balcony from which edicts
were read to the public. The square is completed by the
Baroque Palatine School Building and the Gothic House
of the Panigarola Family, next to each other in a fine
contrast of styles. And finally right before the Loggia
degli Osii is the crowning touch – a charming 16th
century well with columns and trabeation added in the
18th century.

PALAZZO DEI GIURECONSULTI

From this palace, the centuries long seat of the Giureco[
sulti College, came the young men destined to assur
the highest positions of the Milanese state. Angelo Ma[
Medici, who became Pope Pius IV commissioned it fro
Vincenzo Seregni between 1560 and 1564. Anoth
architect, Galeazzo Alessi, designed the façade chara
terized by a double column portico. Between the w[
dows of the upper storey is the Medici family coat
arms crowned by a tiara. Once upon a time the statue
the Spanish king Philip II stood in a niche of the porti
as a reminder of the long Spanish domination of Mila
The French then replaced it with a statue of Brutu
symbol of Republican liberty and virtue, later destroy
by the Austrians in 1799; today a statue of St. Ambro
dominates the façade.

Palazzo dei Giureconsulti; below: **Palazzo della Borsa
designed by Paolo Mezzanotte.**

PALAZZO DELLA BORSA

(The Stock Exchange). The huge proportions of t[
Palazzo della Borsa, symbol of Milan's economic pow[
fittingly represent its dominant position in Italian ec
nomic and financial affairs. Built in 1931 by Pac
Mezzanotte, it is adorned with reliefs and allegorie
statues. Inside, is the three storey Stock Exchange Ha
decorated with stained glass windows and continuous
animated at the change of a digit on the big board.

THE AMBROSIAN
PICTURE GALLERY

In the 1700's Cardinal Federico Borromeo decided
house the precious books and manuscripts he had pa[
stakingly collected all over Europe inside the stately a
simple Ambrosian Palace. Besides the Ambrosian I

Ambrosian Picture Gallery - Fruit Basket by Caravaggio; below: Portrait of a Musician by
Leonardo da Vinci and Portrait of Beatrice d'Este, attributed to Ambrogio de' Predis.

Ambrosian Picture Gallery - The School of Athens, preparatory cartoon by Raphael for the frescoes in the Stanza della Segnatura in the Vatican Palace.

Left: **detail of the Virgin and Child with angels, saints and supplicants by Ambrogio da Fossano, known as Il Bergognone.**

brary, he also added his own private collection paintings, which thus created the core of the futu Ambrosian Picture Gallery. Then in 1796 during th French occupation the finest works in the magnificer collection were carted off as spoils, only some of whi were returned in 1817. The building, which had bee enlarged and transformed over the years, both inside ar out, was heavily bombed during the Second World W and the toll included heavy losses in the paintir collection. Restoration, started just after the war, pr gressed slowly and was only finished in 1959, althoug the final touches to the architecture and the comple rearrangement of the new halls went on until 1966. Th Ambrosian Picture Gallery is today one of Milan's mo visited museums. It is especially noteworthy for i superb treasures from the Lombard and Venetia schools. The vast Hall X, which despite its moder appearance is actually 17th century, contains sever famous cartoons. Outstanding is Raphael's School Athens, which is the only one of the many executed b the artist for his famous fresco cycle in the Vatican. C great interest as well are the cartoons by Pellegrir Tibaldi for the cathedral's stained glass windows an Giulio Romano's for the Battle of Constantine. Titia Tiepolo, Veronese, Dürer, and Brueghel are just a few the other greats whose works may be seen elsewhere i the museum.

THE HOUSE OF THE BORROMEO FAMILY

One of the finest examples of an early 15th century private dwelling, the House of the Borromeo Family was unfortunately lost in the 1943 bombardments. Nevertheless, we may still admire the pointed arch doorway decorated by a graceful motif of an entwining grape vine and oak branch. The inner courtyard of the 15th century two storey building, characterized by pointed windows, is extremely attractive. Inside, the ground floor hall known as the Game Room, is one of the masterpieces of late Gothic painting, even though we can already see some Renaissance touches shyly making their way in. Courtly ladies and gentleman shown playing tarot cards are set amidst a charming landscape in keeping with the new Renaissance naturalistic treatment. The painting has been attributed to various masters such as Pisanello, Giovanni Zenoni, or an unknown follower of Zavattari, but the puzzle is still to be solved.

Right: the lovely marble portal to the House of the Borromeo Family; below: The Tarot Players, an elegant fresco by an unknown, early 15th century master, in a ground-floor room of this palace.

PALAZZO LITTA

Count Bartolomeo Arese commissionned the archite
Richini to design this palace in 1648. Then in the 18
century Balla put on the animated Rococo façade. Insid
the rooms have retained their cold 18th century splendo
the Hall of the Mirrors, one of the most elaborate with i
gilded carvings, the Red Room with its damask line
walls, and the Duchess' Living Room with refine
Chinese art works.

The exterior of Palazzo Litta; below: the Temple of
Victory, built in 1930 to honor Milanese soldiers who
fell in World War I, designed by Giovanni Muzio.

Interior of the church of San Maurizio al Monastero Maggiore.

TEMPLE OF VICTORY

In memory of the sacrifice of over ten thousand Milanese who perished in World War I, this Temple of Victory was erected in 1927-1930 after a design by Giovanni Muzio. The marble sanctuary is in the shape of an octagonal tower with a colonnade below and above a lantern which is lit on holidays.

SAN MAURIZIO

Once annexed to a convent of Benedictine nuns, the church of Monastero Maggiore, also known as San Maurizio, is proof of the high level attained by Lombard Renaissanse architecture. Attributed to Gian Giacomo Dolcebuono, the church has a three storey façade set off by pilaster strips, an extremely simple design repeated

The church of San Maurizio - Bernardino Luini's fresco of the Decapitation of Saint Catherine, dated approximately 1530.

along the left side. The interior, of great impact, has no aisles, but is divided into two sections by a wall separating the public area from the nuns' choir. Both zones are completely covered with frescoes by Leonardo's Lombard follower Bernardino Luini and other Lombard artists of the early 16th century. Hardly ever has church painting better harmonized with its architecture. The frescoes, painted around 1530, are Luini's last work. In the third chapel on the right the master has illustrated scenes from the life of St. Catherine. In the Decapitation of St. Catherine an old tradition has it that the face of the saint is actually a portrait of Countess Bianca Maria di Challant who was herself decapitated in Milan in 1516 in the courtyard of the Sforzesco Castle.

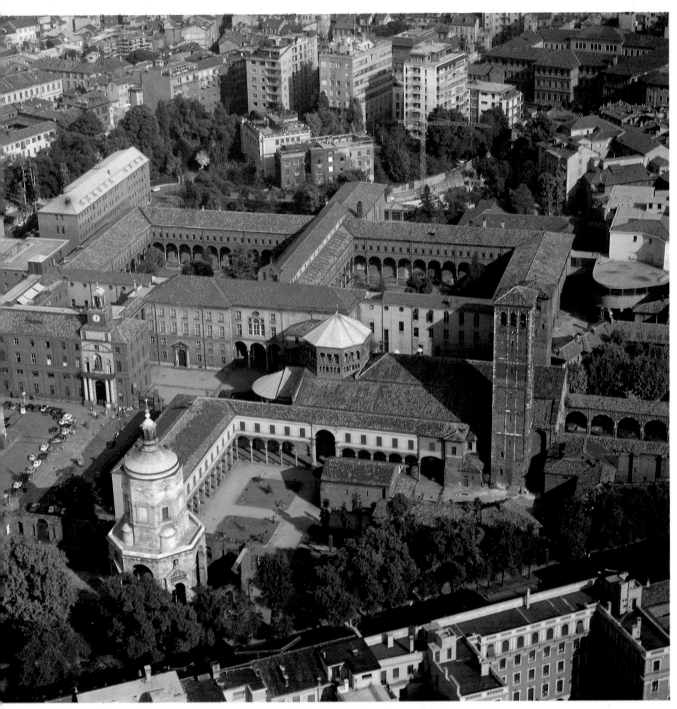

Aerial view of the Sant'Ambrogio complex.

SANT'AMBROGIO

Before plunging into a stylistic discussion of St. Ambrogio, universally acclaimed as the masterpiece of Romanesque architecture in Lombardy and indeed the prototype of all Romanesque architecture in Italy, it might be a good idea to first trace a bit of its history. Milan's best-known church, a basilica, was dedicated to St. Ambrose, the bishop-protector of the city whose mortal remains were buried inside. The whole area around the basilica bears historical significance, for it would appear that this is the site of the palace where in 313 the Emperor Constantine issued his famous Edict granting the early Christians the right to freely practice their religion. It was Ambrose himself who desired that the basilica be built over the site of the Christian burial ground *ad martyres*. The plan of the church consecrated by Ambrose on Januray 13, 386 had single aisles, no

Preceding page: **the porticoed atrium and splendid façade of the Basilica di Sant'Ambrogio;**
above: **the interior of the Basilica di Sant'Ambrogio.**

ansepts, and a single apse, just as it appears today. On pril 5, 397 Ambrose was buried in the church he had unded, between two martyr saints Gervase and Prota- ıs. Four centuries went by and in 789 Archbishop etro added a monastery for Benedictine monks along- le the church. Starting from the 9th century, the urch went through a slow transformation, first when e apse was lengthened and then when the first lltower, the one on the left known as the Monks' ⸰wer, was put up. Later on, in the middle of the 10th ntury, the nave and aisles were rebuilt and the second lltower called the Rectors' Tower went up on the left le. In 1150 the narthex (porch preceding the church) ıs rebuilt to replace the original one commissioned by rchbishop Ansperto. By this time the church had taken the pure Romanesque look it has retained up to this ry day, despite Bramante's Renaissance touches in the ctory and cloisters. Not even the damage caused by the gust 1943 bombing could mar such incredible harmony. e basilica is basically the same building which wit- ssed the coronations of the Holy Roman emperors and ceived the earthly remains of numerous Christian

martyrs in addition to St. Ambrose, as well as those of kings renowned throughout the Middle Ages, such as Pippin, Bernard, Ludovico II and Lotarius. As if to conceal a part of its spartan loveliness, St. Ambrogio's façade is half hidden by the brick wall of the narthex; only the upper part and the two belltowers are visible. How different they are: the one on the right is so simple and plain, while the one on the left sports a fine example of Lombard decorative style with the subtle rhythm of the vertical pilaster strips contrasted by the horizontal accents of the arched corbel tables (rows of arch motifs). As soon as we step into the atrium we are struck by the harmonious proportions of the single façade composed of a five part arch above the three bays of the narthex which gracefully emphasize the slope of the gable. All the decorative elements, pilaster strips, openings, and corbel tables bestow a note of color to the stately architectural structure. The equally stately interior was ahead of its time in the use of what would later be common Roma- nesque elements, especially in Lombard architecture, such as vaulted bays, a raised choir, and the alternation of heavy and light piers down the nave.

The Golden Altarpiece or Paliotto, 9th century master-piece by Master Volvinio; left: detail of the canopy and Ciborium.

Interior – The overpowering and majestic effect of the chur interior is achieved by an extremely careful definition of spa i.e. the aisles are divided from the nave into three bays cover by ribbed vaults and all of the architectural and decorati elements are emphasized by the color contrast of the red br outline against the light-colored walls. Among the numero works of art inside the church, the best known is the Gold Altar which Archbishop Angilberto commissioned from Mas Volvinio during the early 9th century. A unique masterpiece Carolingian craftsmanship, the altar is composed of four g and silver panels encrusted with gem stones, pearls, ser precious stones, and enamels. The altar stands beneath t Ciborium of four red porphyry Roman columns supporting canopy. The painted stucco decorations on the four sides canopy depict the glory of Christ and St. Ambrose.

The Pusterla di Sant'Ambrogio.

PUSTERLA DI SANT'AMBROGIO

t. Ambrose Gateway) – The famous "pusterla" is ctually an imposing double arch gateway built in 1171 ithin the medieval city walls. On one of the double çades is a tabernacle with statues of Sts. Ambrose, Gervase, and Protasius. Every year on St. Ambroses's feast-day in December, a colorful fair is held here – one of the rare traditions that has withstood the onslaught of Progress.

The exterior of the church of Santa Maria della Grazie; opposite page: the Tribune by Bramante.

SANTA MARIA DELLE GRAZIE

The unique blend of simple elegant Tuscan architectural forms and colorful Lombard decorative motifs produced an extraordinary offspring: the church of Santa Maria delle Grazie. In 1463, a captain in Francesco Sforza's army, Gaspare Vimercati, donated a plot of land to the Domenican order. On the site was a chapel adorned with a fresco of the Virgin, the so-called Madonna delle Grazie. The monks commissioned Guiniforte Solari to build a church and monastery on the plot, and ground was broken on September 10, 1463. The church that Solari built between 1466 and 1490 is a typical example of the transition stage between Gothic and Renaissance, as can be seen in the Lombard style gabled façade decorated with pilaster strips and pierced by a single opening below and several niches above. Only the gabled portal belongs to the period when the Renaissance architect Bramante was involved in the work. The church was just about ready – the presbytery and apse had already been finished – when the new ruler of Milan, Ludovico il Moro, ordered it enlarged. Both presbytery

and apse were torn down so that Donato Bramante cou put up his own design for the huge apse. It was begun March 1492 and when it was completed in 1497 Ludovi had his wife, Beatrice d'Este, buried there. Bramante great tribune was a lesson in Renaissance architecture the artists of Lombardy, even though his idea of thr apses radiating from a square is actually based on a older building (the Parma Cathedral). Nevertheless, v must not fail to mention that the great Florenti architect of the Early Renaissance, Brunelleschi, great influenced Bramante's concept of simple, perfectly pr portioned, harmonious space. From the outside t tribune looks like a giant wheel resting upon a cube. T decorative effect is enhanced by the double colun arcade encircling the top part of the dome and the use rectangular windows alternating with pilasters cut in the lower level. Geometric patterns in brickwork ma an attractive contrast against the neutral color of t wall surface. All of these elements combine to give sense of spatial grandeur satisfying both eye and spir

Bartholomew   Andrew   Peter   John   Jesus   Thomas   Philip   Matthew   Thaddeus   Simon

James the Less   Judas   James the Great

The Last Supper by Leonardo da Vinci.

LEONARDO'S LAST SUPPER

The eighteen years that Leonardo da Vinci spent at the court of Ludovico il Moro had such an impact on the history of Lombard art that the whole 16th century was affected. Leonardo started work on the fresco – judged by many the genius's greatest work – in 1496 when he received a commission from Ludovico who, after having enlarged the church of Santa Maria delle Grazie, decided to enlarge and decorate the Refectory (Dining Hall) of the adjacent Dominican monastery. Leonardo's snailpace work on the fresco soon became legendary. In fact, in a letter sent by Ludovico to Marchesino Stampa dated June 29, 1497, Ludovico specifies that "we have made the heartfelt decision... to urge Leonardo the Florentine to finish the work he has undertaken in the Refectory of Santa Maria delle Grazie." By then the Last Supper was probably awaiting only the finishing touches. Leonardo painted it using an unconventional technique, sometimes without letting go of a paintbrush the whole day long, other times not picking up a paintbrush for days at a time. Unfortunately, this technique involving the use of tempera paint over a double layer of plaster (rather than true fresco pigment which becomes part of the wall itself)

proved faulty, and the fresco, which could not withstand the dampness of the wall it was painted on, was soon decaying. By 1568, the writer-artist Vasari could already write of a "striking stain". This was due to moisture collecting under the paint, causing the pigment layer to fall off, the formation of saltpetre and the spreading of mold. These inherent defects were worsened by the tampering of French mercenary troops in the 16th century followed by Napoleon's soldiers in the 18th century. Emerging miraculously unscathed from the August 1943 bombings which meanwhile had completely destroyed the Refectory, the Last Supper was given the best of modern restoration treatment to save it from total ruin (numerous past attempts had miserably failed). Leonardo put great emphasis on the depth out of which the twilight emanates to bathe the figures in its uniform glow. The apostles are placed in groups of three along the horizontal plane of the table whose center is the fixed point of the Christ figure. All the lines of the composition converge on Him, including the gestures and glances of the apostles, each of whom is portrayed reacting differently according to his psychological state, to the words of Christ.

53

The Crucifixion, fresco by Giovanni Donato Montorfano, on the wall opposite Leonardo's Last Supper; left: the interior of Santa Maria delle Grazie; following page: cloister, traditionally attributed to Donato Bramante, with the impressive Tribune above.

Interior – The interior, like the outside of the church, is rich satisfying in its magnificently conceived contrast of the nave Gothic purity and the tribune's Renaissance decorativenes Guiniforte Solari designed the nave with its Gothic sty pointed arches. The strong downward thrust of the arche brusquely interrupted where the pilaster strips join the dec rated capitals of the columns, creates a feeling of gre spaciousness in the nave. The rhythmic procession of colum leads us to Bramante's tribune. The inside of the cube with i strictly geometric partition of space, appears fragmented the use of colorful decorative motifs. The four huge arches, o for each side of the cube, join the lower spaced to the dome, means of pendentives. The end arch opens into the presbyter whereas the other two form giant niches on either side of t choir. The painted decoration is extremely simple, and it is the extreme simplicity of the geometrical motifs, that t originality of Bramante's conception lies. Only three design the circle, the square, and the spoked wheel, are used, and th are harmoniously repeated.

54

Museum of Science and Technology - The Leonardo da Vinci Gallery.

MUSEUM OF SCIENCE AND TECHNOLOGY

The National Museum of Science and Technology, named after Leonardo da Vinci and located inside the 16th century San Vittore Monastery, is unique in Italy. Founded in 1953, its aim is to spread the history of scientific thought and technological-industrial breakthroughs through documentation comprising drawings, machines, models, historical relics, and inventions. Among the fascinating exhibits are Ravizza's famous proto-typewriter of 1885, precursor of the modern typewriter, a late 19th century steam generator unit, carriag-es, velocipedes, and sewing machines to name just a fe... The Watch and Clock Exhibit is outstanding for its va... collection of time devices ranging from the earlie... sundials and water clocks right up to the latest mode... Of course, Leonardo da Vinci's inventions are give... special emphasis. A room is dedicated to drawing... models, reproductions, and giant photos of the i... ventions of the great genius. A giant reproduction ... Leonardo's self-portrait engraved on a glass partitic... greets the visitor at the entrance to the exhibit.

Museum of Science and Technology - Two rooms dedicated to transportation.

Largo Cairoli with the Sforzesco Castle in the background.

LARGO CAIROLI

The bustling Via Dante, a fashionable shopping street leads into Largo Cairoli, dominated by the imposing Monument to Garibaldi, sculpted by Ettore Ximenes in 1895. The bronze figures on the pedestal symbolize Revolution and Liberty. From either side of the monument extend the arms of the treeshaded boulevard, Fo Buonaparte, flanking the Sforzesco Castle in its sen circular embrace. Behind the monument the short V Beltrami leads right into the pleasantly landscap Piazza Castello.

Aerial view of the Sforzesco Castle.

THE SFORZESCO CASTLE

We do not know the name of the architect who first conceived this overpowering brickwork complex, but it was probably begun when Galeazzo Visconti had a castle built along the Roman walls near the city gate named after Jupiter; thus the castle was popularly known as the castle of the Jupiter Gate. The complex, with several constructions on the inside, was built in the shape of a huge rectangle around a vast inner courtyard facing the city. From the very beginning, the castle was the scene of both happy and not so happy events. Bernabò Visconti was kept prisoner there in 1385 and another great of the celebrated family, Filippo Maria, was born there in 1392. The citadel, better fortified by Giovanni Maria, became the Viscontis' permanent residence. Filippo Maria, embellished it, commissioning even the great Florentine architect Brunelleschi to do some of the work. During the upheavals which followed the death of Filippo Maria, the newborn Ambrosian Republic decreed the complete destruction of the stronghold, though luckily the demolition was only partially carried out. The new lord of the city, Francesco Sforza, disregarded the pact he had signed on February 26, 1450 with representatives of the Milanese citizenry. In the pact he had agreed to have the gloomy Visconti fortress torn down, instead he commis-

sioned Giovanni da Milano to rebuild the destroyed parts. Giovanni was succeeded by Filarete who designed the tower rising midway at the entrance, and then by Gadio da Cremona who managed to speed up the work so that upon Francesco Sforza's death on March 8, 1466 the castle was practically finished. Work on finishing the exterior and decorating the interior went on simultaneously. Over the years the castle was becoming one of the most sumptuous royal places in all of Northern Italy. The height of splendor was reached when Ludovico il Moro summoned Bramante and Leonardo to take part in the project. The castle could thus make a storybook setting for Gian Galeazzo's wedding to Isabella d'Aragon in December 1488 and Ludovico's to Beatrice d'Este in January 1491. All this architectural wonder was not enough to withstand the French invasion of 1499 and the castle fell into enemy hands. It was reconquered by Massimiliano Sforza in 1513 but only for a short time since Massimiliano, blocked in Milan by François I's French troops, was forced to retreat. In 1525 the castle was subjected to still another siege, this one directed against the imperial troops of Francesco II Sforza who had taken shelter inside. The greatest fortifications, however, were those erected during the 1560's when

59

Largo Cairoli by night, with the monument to Giuseppe Garibaldi by Ettore Ximenes in the foreground and the Sforzesco Castle in the back; following page: Filarete's Tower also known as the Clock Tower, at the entrance to the Castle.

fortress was in such a terrible state that a comple demolition was proposed. Luckily, the Lombard Histo ical Society stepped in and prevented further tamperin Shortly afterwards, a total restoration project wa drawn up by Luca Beltrami and in 1895 work got und way. Unhappily, as was the case for most of th monuments in Milan, August of 1943 brought bombs ar devastation to the Sforzesco Castle, though the damag was soon patched up in the years immediately followir the war. The Sforzesco Castle lies in the very heart Milan, not only for its geographical position, but also f its great importance to the Milanese. Its effect majestic and overpowering. The façade with Filarete Tower in the middle is flanked by a cylindrical tower either end. Of rusticated stone, they are crenelated ar adorned with a plaque bearing the famous snake mot representing the Visconti and Sforza families. You mig have noticed the snake elsewhere in Milan – it is th trademark of one of Italy's biggest automobile man facturers which, needless to say, is a Milanese firm. Th two corner towers, called the Tower of the Falconers ar the Castellana or Treasury Tower, look somewhat squ and cumbersome, although the huge windows do contri ute to lighten the effect. On the right, the Ludovico Moro Drawbridge spans the moat and leads to th courtyard around which Ludovico il Moro's chambe were located; the loggia has been attributed to Br mante, Here, in one of the little rooms overlooking th moat, Ludovico is said to have sat in mourning when h wife Beatrice d'Este died. Crossing the drawbridge over the moat, we enter the inner courtyard. It is a almost overwhelming experience to visit the castle wit its remarkable masterpieces of art in their equal remarkable history-filled setting.

Vincenzo Seregni designed six bulwarks laid out like points of a star around the fortress, completed towards the end of the 16th century. Thereafter a moat was dug and six separate ravelins, i.e. masonry elements, were put up before the gates for defense. The grandiose fortress thus acquired the shape of a twelve pointed star. Even though the castle never witnessed great military events, its history is far from uneventful. Conquered in 1733 by Carlo Emanuele III of Savoy, it later fell under Spanish and in 1796 French domination. On June 17, 1800 it was abandoned by the Austrians; Napoleon immediately had the citadel demolished, and thus only the actual Sforzesco Castle was left standing. Fourteen years later the castle once more served as barracks for the Austrian troops and it was from here that Radetzky commanded the cannon fire over the city during the five days of insurrection in 1848. The Austrian general ordered the total demolition of the corner towers, and in 1880 the

Filarete's Tower – When in 1452, the Florentine Antonio Pietro Averulino, known as Filarete, was summoned to th Sforza Court in Milan, the castle had already been bad damaged and was on the point of being torn down. Filaret commissioned with the restoration project, also designed th distinctive tower in the middle of the entrance façade. U fortunately, the tower toppled on June 23, 1527 when th gunpowder stored inside it blew up. As part of the tot restoration project carried out by the Milanese architect Luc Beltrami at the turn of the 20th century, Filarete's tower wa rebuilt according to what the original was supposed to hav been like. On September 24, 1904, it was reborn, 227 feet ta square in shape, replete with recessed storeys. Above th entrance gate is Secchi's marble bas-relief portraying Umber I on horseback, put up in memory of the King's assassinatio Just below the first crenelation amidst the huge coats of arm is a statue representing St. Ambrose; still higher up is a hug clock. On either side of the tower stretches a majestic red bric curtain whose only decoration consists of the two part windov piercing it. Filarete's tower is a prime example of the 19t century passion for restoring works in medieval and Renai sance styles (actually we learn more about the 19th centur from these "faithful reconstructions" than we do about th originals). Nevertheless, the tower is still a distinctive featur of Milan.

Sforzesco Castle - Detail of the drawbridge.

Drawbridge and training grounds – After crossing the drawbridge and the gateway cut into Filarete's Tower, we reach the vast courtyard known as Piazza d'Armi (the Weapon Court). Today it looks like a quiet, nicely-landscaped lawn, but it must have looked rather different when it was being used as training grounds for the Sforza army. The modern buildings by the wall house the City Museums, the Art Library, and the Bertarelli Prints and Drawing Collection. Looking carefully, one can pick out signs of buildings that are no longer standing,

such as a piece of the Renaissance courtyard with traces of fresco and another belonging to a second courtyard of the same period with brickwork decoration. Opposite Filarete's Tower a statue of St. John Nepomuceno, protector of bridge commissioned from Giovanni Dugani in 1729 by one of the Viscontis. Beyond the covered bridge is the tower of Bona Savoia that the widow of Galeazzo Maria Sforza had built 1477 as protection from the insidious plotting of Ludovico Moro.

Two views of the Training Grounds.

The Castle Museums - Detail of the fresco cycle from the Roccabianca Castle, depicting the life of Griselda, by an anonymous 15th century master; opposite page: the Rondanini Pietà, Michelangelo's last, unfinished masterpiece.

Art Museums – These museums are the pride of the castle and indeed of the whole city. The permanent exhibition was set up only in 1954-1963 by the architects Rogers-Nathan, Barbiano di Belgioios, and Peressutti. Among the numerous works of art on exhibit in the Museums, one of the most worthy of note is the Rondanini Pietà, Michelangelo's last work; he was working on it just before he died. The sculpture, which rests upon a late Roman funerary slab, was purchased by the City of Milan from the private collection of the Marquis Rondanini of Rome in 1952. There is something medieval and at the same time contemporary about the piece which lifts it from its chronologically Renaissance conception – a timeless masterpiece is born from the conquest of form towards pure spiritual content. The two gaunt figures are as if fused together in a last desperate embrace. Another famous masterpiece on exhibit is the Funerary Monument of Bernabò Visconti by Bonino da Campio. The Swiss artist, whose work is dated 1357, managed to convey a feeling of contained strength in the sturdy figures of horse and rider. One of the halls houses three very important fresco cycles of the Lombard school. The loveliest of all illustrates the Story of Griselda taken from one of Boccaccio's novellas. The frescoes originally came from a room in the Roccabianca Castle, south of Milan, and were painted between 1446 and 1460 by an anonymous master close to Nicolò da Varallo. They were commissioned by Pier Maria Rossi, commander in the Visconti army, friend of Lorenzo the Magnificent, and nobleman of Parma, in honor of his beloved, the renowned beauty Bianca Pellegrini d'Arluno.

The Castle Museums - Preceding page: **Funeral Monument to Bernabò Visconti by Bonino da Campione;** above: **the Weapons Collection room;** right: **6th century Byzantine marble bust, supposedly the Empress Teodora.**

[D]ucal Court and Rocchetta Courtyard – The door surmonted [b]y a huge Sforza coat of arms leads us to the Ducal Court [w]here the art museums are located. The vestibule we pass [th]rough before reaching the court is full of sculpture and the [si]nopia (preparatory drawing) of a remarkable late 15th [ce]ntury fresco by an anonymous Lombard master. The fresco [(c]urrently in the museum warehouse) depicts Christ crucified [am]idst saints and Ambrosino da Longhignana who was Lord of [th]e Castle to Galeazzo Maria Sforza first and then to Bona di [Sa]voia. The courtyard is enclosed on three sides by a structure [w]ith two rows of pointed windows framed in brick. The lawn is [la]ndscaped in typical Italian style with architectural fragments [st]rewn about the grass. During times of great danger, the [Sf]orza used to seek shelter in the Rocchetta, which was felt to [b]e one of the safest spots in the whole castle. Here too there [ar]e two rows of pointed windows, but the overall effect is [li]ghtened by the arcading below which opens out on three sides. [Th]e portico had a trio of architetcts: the Florentine Benedetto [Fe]rrini who designed the one in the middle, Filarete, who [de]signed the one in front and Bernardino da Corte who is [re]sponsible for the left one (which, however, was actually [fin]ished by Bramante).

The Castle Museums - Above, from the left: the city's standard, a fine embroidery shows Saint Ambrose banishing the Aryans and other scenes from his life; Egyptian funerary figurine; below: ceramics from Urbino and Milan, in the Chinese style.

The Sforzesco Castle - Ducal Court; below: some of the display cases in the Museum of Musical
Instruments and a gilded 17th century armchair.

The Park which extends behind the Sforzesco Castle: opposite page: Francesco Barzaghi's monument to Napoleon III in the park.

THE PARK

The park that the Milanese love to walk about and enjoy for its charming landscaping is actually only a tiny part of what once belonged to the Sforza family. The present landscaping was conceived in 1893 by the architect Alemagna who laid out the 117 acre garden in the typical English style. Broad winding pathways intersect to form charming lawns shaded by thick clumps of trees. Just beyond the hill called Tordo Knoll is the monument to Napoleon III by Francesco Barzaghi in 1881. The statue was transported here from its original site in the Senate Building in 1927 and at that time set on a huge base adorned with bas-reliefs. One portrays the Battle of Magenta with the assault of the Zouaves and the hunter of Vincennes, while the other shows Napoleon and Vittorio Emanuele II entering Milan. The park does not end here: the Palace of Art, permanent headquarters for the Tri-annual Decorative Art Show and the old arena or City Stadium, elliptical in shape, Neo-Classical in style built by Luigi Canonica in 1806, are also within the park limits.

Above and following page: **the Arch of Peace built to plans by Luigi Cagnola at the beginning of the last century.**

THE ARCH OF PEACE

The arch framing the Sforzesco Castle in the background calls up memories of when Vittorio Emanuele and Napoleon III passed under it. The 73 foot high arch was begun during the fall of 1807 on the model of the wood and canvas one which had been erected in honor of Viceroy Eugène Beauharnais the year before at Porta Orientale. Construction was suspended in 1808 on account of political events, and not resumed until 1826 under the enlightened intervention of the Austrian emperor Franz I who decided to call it the Arch of Peace as a reminder of the peace which finally united all of Europe after the Napoleonic storm had blown over. The architect Luigi Cagnola was commissioned with the project and after his death in 1833 Francesco Londonio and Francesco Peverelli took over where he had left off. It took five years to complete the work and on September 10, 1838 in the presence of Ferdinand I, Emperor of Austria and King of the Lombard and Venetian provinces, the arch was officially inaugurated. The Corinthian arch is built out of Baveno granite (Baveno is near Milan) but completely lined with Crévola marble. The arch, li its Roman precedecessors, is actually composed of thr arches with four huge fluted columns supporting a frie of the same proportions. Above, on either side, are t inscriptions commemorating the entrance of Napole III and Vittorio Emanuele II into Milan which in 18 replaced the original exalting Franz I and Ferdinand Atop the frieze is the bronze Chariot of Peace dra by six steeds by Abbondio Sangiorgio, and four ad tional Victories astride horses, one on each corn by Giovanni Putti. The seated marble figures benea the Victories represent the four main rivers of t Lombardy and Veneto regions: the Po, the Ticino, t Adige, and the Tagliamento. The rest of the arch covered with reliefs portraying the highlights of t restoration followed by the Fall of Napoleon Bonapart The effectiveness of the whole, simple as to form a complex as to decoration, makes the Arch of Peace o of the most admirable examples of Neo-Classical art Milan.

The interior of the church at the Charterhouse of Garegnano dedicated to Santa Maria Assunta;
opposite page: **the façade of the church.**

THE CHARTERHOUSE OF GAREGNANO

The original building on the site of the present-day Charterhouse was commissioned by the archbishop of Milan, Giovanni Visconti, in 1349. The writer Petrarch, owner of a nearby villa, often visited the Charterhouse to converse with the Carthusian monks. Between 1562 and 1603 the building was replaced with the present one and a monastery, almost completely destroyed in 1782. The church reflects the Baroque period with its showy elliptical vestibule and richly adorned tripart façade. The interior is much more attractive. Designed by Vincenzo Seregni, but restored by Ambrogio Annoni, it has an aisleless nave leading to an apsed presbytery topped by a dome. The nave walls, covered with remarkable vaulting, are divided into bays by broad arches separated by pilaster strips – the overall effect is one of great tranquility. The walls are frescoed with scenes narrating the foundation of the order, considered the masterpiece of their painter, Daniele Crispi, who displayed great narrative skill and fine handling of color in the work. One of the scenes, the first to the right, depicting the funeral of Diocrès, was greatly appreciated by Lord Byron who would stand and admire it for hours on end. In the sixth scene on the left wall we have a self-portrait of Crispi who chose to depict himself as the servant playing a horn. Here in the left corner we can also see the painter's signature and the date: 1629. This harmonious blending of architecture and decoration makes the church a richly rewarding experience.

The Brera Palace, home of the famous picture gallery and other important cultural institutions.

THE BRERA PICTURE GALLERY

On a charming street in old Milan, Via Brera, stands the Brera Palace at number 28, flanked by other elegant 18th century places. It was built on the site of what was once the 14th century Monastery of the Humiliated Monks. When the order was suppressed, the monastery was taken over by the Jesuits (in 1572) who proceeded to install their schools in the building until 1591 when they commissioned the architect Martino Bassi to build a new and more grandiose college. Starting in 1615 the project was continued by Francesco Maria Richini, although it was not completed until 1773. Richini's great inventiveness is best seen in the wonderful rectangular courtyard enhanced by a stately two storey colonnade of slender columns. The chiaroscuro effect, enhanced by the contrast of the filled and empty spaces, is attained by a double arcade of paired columns. In the center of the courtyard is a bronze statue that Antonio Cano executed in 1809 representing Napoleon. The emperor idealized according to classical canons as a nude, your god, holding a sceptor in his right hand and a perso ification of Victory in his left. Across the courtyard v come to the double staircase which leads to the secor floor and the entrance to the celebrated Painting M seum (Pinacoteca). The Brera, one of Italy's finest, h an outstanding collection covering especially the Lor bard and Venetian schools. The museum was founde during the Napoleonic period, in 1803, for the most pa as a result of the good offices of Francesco Melzi, vi president of the Republic, and the painter Giusep Bossi, who gathered works from suppressed religio institutions and secularized churches, all of which we supposed to be left to the Fine Arts Academy f

The inside courtyard of the Brera Palace with the fine portico and two-storey colonnade by Ricchini; right: Monument to Napoleon as Mars the Peacemaker, cast in bronze by Francesco and Luigi Righetti, from a model by Antonio Canova.

aching purposes. Opened to the public in 1805, the useum collection was enriched by a century of acquisins and bequests. Badly damaged by bombs in August 43, it was rebuilt according to modern criteria by odigliani, Portaluppi, and Wittgens who completed the novations in 1950. The collection's range is amazing: m Luini's fresco cycle from Villa Pelucca to Gaudenzio rrari's from St. Maria della Pace, from Giovanni da lano's exquisite 14th century panels to Veronese's ge 17th century canvases, from Tintoretto's dramatic discovery of St. Mark's Body to Mantegna's underted Dead Christ, from the eight frescoes from the nigarola House by Bramante and the same artist's rist Bound at the Columns to the masterpieces by phael and Piero della Francesca. And to think these e only some of the famous names in Brera.

The Brera Picture Gallery - Detail of St. Mark Preaching in Egypt by Gentile and Giovanni Bellini; below: Pietà by Giovanni Bellini and the Dead Christ by Andrea Mantegna; following page: The Marriage of the Virgin by Raphael.

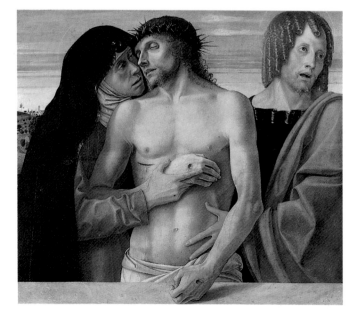

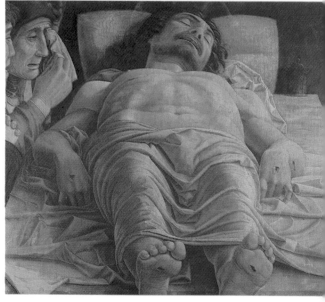

Brera Picture Gallery - Preceding page: **Virgin with Child, Angels and Saints and Federico da Montefeltro by Piero della Francesca**; above: **Madonna del Roseto by Bernardino Luini**; right: **The Martyrdom of Saint Sebastian by Vincenzo Foppa**; below: **The Discovery of the Body of Saint Mark by Tintoretto and Jesus in the Garden of Gethsemane by Veronese**.

The façade of the Church of San Simpliciano.

SAN SIMPLICIANO

This church, one of the oldest in Milan, has great sentimental value for the Milanese, who according to legend were supposed to have received aid from the three saints buried here (Martirius, Sisinius, and Alexander, martyrs of Anaunia) enabling them to defeat Frederick Barbarossa in the Battle of Legnano in 1176. The basilica, built, in the 4th century, possibly on the site of a pagan cemetery, was commissioned by St. Ambrose, though it was finished by his successor, St. Simplician. Restored at the beginning of the 7th century by the Lombard Kings Agilulf and Adaloald, the church was unfortunately tampered with as a result of the numerous restorations and changes made over the years. Today, we can still admire the typically 12th century features left despite even more recent tampering. The façade typically Lombard with its sloping roof and three sto portals which open from below (the two side on however, are modern restorations). Above, slender lumns divide the windows cut into the façade. Every ye on May 29 the church is the setting for a pictures ceremony to celebrate the victory of Legnano. Legend fact has it that on that day three snow white doves to flight from the tombs of the three martyrs and alight on the altar of the battle cart around which the bat was raging. Thus, every year in the piazza adjoining t church a host of white doves is launched into the air memory of the victory at Legnano which reaffirm Milan's freedom.

General view and details of the Monumental Cemetery.

MONUMENTAL CEMETERY

esigned by the architect Maciachini in the Lombard
othic style, Milan's celebrated Monumental Cemetery
as inaugurated in 1866. Spread out over a vast area
vering more than 50 acres, the cemetery is full of
apels, commemorative monuments, busts and pieces of
atuary, many of which are of great artistic value.
side the main building is the hall known as the city's
antheon which contains, among others, the sarcoph-
;us of the Italian writer Manzoni. Busts of famous
storical figures and the names of well-known native
d honorary Milanese decorate the walls. The Monu-
ental Cemetery is truly unique in all of Italy for the
mber and quality of its funerary monuments.

VIA MANZONI

Long ago called Garden Lane, Via Manzoni is today on of the most aristocratic streets in the city. All th buildings lining it are connected with historical event Two of the most important are the Neo-Classical buildir at the corner of Via Verdi, where the followers Mazzini, the great Italian patriot, used to meet in th Circolo dell'Unione and the Café Cova, meetingplace intellectuals in the second half of the 19th century.

Left: **a view of Via Manzoni;** *below:* **the entrance to the Poldi-Pezzoli Museum;** *opposite page:* **Portrait of a Lady by Antonio del Pollaiolo.**

THE POLDI-PEZZOLI MUSEUM

It really seems as though every building in Milan is actually a museum – along the fashionable thoroughfare, Via Manzoni, at number 12, we find the Poldi-Pezzoli Museum. Originally the building was the home of the titled art collector Gian Giacomo Poldi-Pezzoli. When he died in 1879 he left all the collections he had so lovingly assembled in his own home to a foundation set up for th benefit of the general public. Although seriously dam aged during the last war, the museum was quick restored and today, while scrupulously adhering to th most modern museum criteria, it has managed to pr serve the feeling of a 19th century private collection

The elegant shops along Via Montenapoleone.

VIA MONTENAPOLEONE

Milan, like the other great capitals worldover, is not ju
art and history. Milan too has fashionable streets whe
"in" people flock to shop and meet. Via Montenapol
one, one of Milan's most elegant thoroughfares, is line
with luxurious boutiques, antique shops, tearooms an
cafés. All along the street are the ateliers of the to
Milanese designers. Not surprisingly, Milan now ranks a
one of Europe's fashion capitals, just like Paris, Rom
and Florence.

The Porta Nuova Arches; right: the Roman stele with busts of the cloth merchant, Vezzio and his family set inside a supporting arch.

ORTA NUOVA ARCHES

oday unfortunately squashed between modern buildings ese black and white marble arches originally belonged the walls built between 1156 and 1158 to defend the ty from Barbarossa's assaults. The arches were rebuilt 1171 as they are today, although they did undergo storation in 1861. Inside the barrel vaults, recent cavations have turned up pieces of Roman funerary aques. A curiosity – one of the niches, according to the scription below it, contains the busts of the relatives of certain Vezzio, cloth merchant.

The façade of the church of Sant'Angelo and the Pirelli Skyscraper.

SANT'ANGELO

The façade of the church of the Franciscan order, Sant'Angelo, was conceived by the architect Domenico Giunti in the post-Renaissance Mannerist style of the late 16th century. Built between 1552 and 1584, the church has a façade divided in two by a false portico resting on columns. The interior, a single vast space uncluttered by aisles and covered by barrel vaults, is lined with chapels richly adorned with paintings and stucco decoration.

PIAZZA DELLA REPUBBLIC&

Piazza della Repubblica, site of an eternal traffic jan extends over the area of the old railway station. Fou skyscrapers, including the two "twin towers" buì during the 'sixties border on this square with i tree-lined lawns and Cascella's 1974 monument to Gì seppe Mazzini in the center. The building on the righ with Via Pisani in the background, was built in 1954; it 114 meters tall and is known as "Milan's Skyscraper

The front of the Central Railway Station.

CENTRAL RAILWAY STATION

The enormous Piazza d'Aosta is dominated by the Pirelli skyscraper which was built in 1955-60 over the site of the original, tiny Pirelli plant that was put up in 1872. This 127 meter high building currently houses the offices of the Lombard Regional Government. The Piazza is the setting for the Central Railway Station. Designed by Stacchini it was officially inaugurated on May 15, 1931, although the original design dates back to 1906. It is impossible to classify this odd style – a hodgepodge of ornamentation, statuary and decoration. The façade, 673 feet long, is composed of a tall jutting center element with three huge arches plus wings on either side also with arches. The whole enormous porch is an entranceway to the 91 foot high lobby where train tickets are sold. From the lobby decorated with reliefs and statuary, two majestic staircases – lead to the 18 track, roofed in area where the trains arrive and depart. Milan is an important junction for rail traffic coming from outside Italy or originating in Italy headed anywhere down the long narrow Italian peninsula.

The church of San Carlo al Corso; below: the church of San Babila.

SAN CARLO AL CORSO

In the heart of old Milan a stately Classical touch i unexpectedly given by the church of San Carlo al Corso The building, designed by Amati, was put up betwee 1832 and 1847 while the distinctive vaulted dome designed by Felice Pizzagalli was erected in 1844 Everything recalls the Classical style, from the protruc ing porch upon which a dedication to St. Carlo Borrome is carved to the three-sided colonnade embracing th square.

PIAZZA SAN BABILA

Today Piazza San Babila looks very different from how i appeared just a few years ago – new buildings have bee springing up like mushrooms and the church of Sa Babila is almost lost amidst them. The church we se today was built about the end of the 11th century probably on the site of the pre-existing 5th centur basilica founded by St. Lawrence, although it has bee considerably altered over the centuries.

Palazzo Serbelloni; right: **the grand staircase in Palazzo Castiglioni, fine example of Art Nouveau architecture.**

CORSO VENEZIA

...any well-known historical buildings are located along ...orso Venezia, originally called the "East Gate Road". ...umber 11 houses what was once the Bishop's Seminary ...unded by St. Carlo Borromeo in 1564. Of great note is ...e heavy Baroque rusticated stone portal adorned with ...pair of caryatids, designed by Richini in 1652. Farther ..., we come to the 17th century Serbelloni Palace later ...tered in the "more uptodate" Neo-Classical style in ...'93. The building, which today houses the Press Club, ...mbers among its celebrated guests of the past Napo... ...on in 1796, Metternich, Vittorio Emanuele II king of ...aly, and Napoleon III. On the lefthand side at Corso ...enezia 47, is one of the finest art nouveau buildings in ...ilan, the Castiglioni Palace designed by Giuseppe ...ommaruga. Number 40, the Saporiti Palace was de... ...gned in 1812 in the Neo-Classical style by Giovanni ...erego, who decorated the façade with statuary and a ...lonnade.

Villa Reale; below: Monument to Antonio Stoppani by Francesco Confalonieri in the Public Gardens.

VILLA REALE

Another example, this time rather gaudy, of Neo Classical in Milan, the Villa Reale was designed in 179 by Leopoldo Pollack for Count Ludovico di Barbiano Belgioioso. Among the famous people who have lived the villa are Napoleon and his wife Josephine, Vicerc Beauharnais, and General Radetzky. The façade ove looking the garden deserves special attention – the pla of light created by the agitated forms conveys a pictu esque effect. The two basreliefs depicting the Chariots Day and Night and statues on the roof are by Dei.

PUBLIC GARDENS

The gardens, a green oasis in downtown Milan, we designed by Piermarini between 1783 and 1786, and the later enlarged by order of the Austrian emperor Fra Joseph in 1857. Giuseppe Balzaretto and Alemagr turned them into English style gardens dotted with bus of famous men including a bronze of Giacosa ar Confalonieri's statue of Antonio Rosmini. Rather sma only 42 acres, the park is nevertheless one of Milan most pleasant. The gardens are also home to the 20.0(square meter Zoo, one of the largest in Italy.

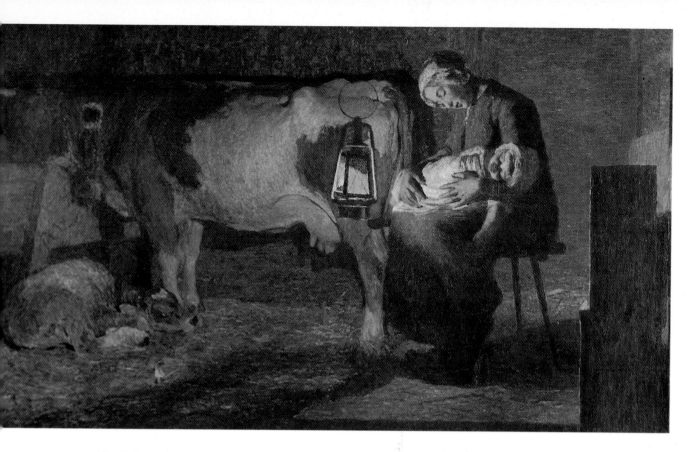

The Gallery of Modern Art - Two Mothers by Giovanni Segantini; below: **The Fisherboy, bronze sculpture by Vincenzo Gemito.**

THE GALLERY OF MODERN ART

ow owned by the city of Milan, the Villa Reale houses
e of the finest Italian collections of modern art, with a
ecial emphasis on 19th century Lombard painting. The
useum came into being in 1868 with the Marchesi
gliani bequest which was soon broadened by other
orks either willed or donated to the museum. Both
intings and sculpture cover a wide range of periods
om divisionismo to futurism. Antonio Canova, Domen-
o Induno, Giovanni Fattori, Silvestro Lega are some of
e Italian masters displayed, while the French are
presented by Sisley, Gauguin, Manet, Van Gogh,
enoir and Cézanne. Lesser known to the non-Italian
blic, but worthy of a good look, are the painting by
ovanni Segantini, whose memorable renderings of
mple scenes of everyday life emanate a feeling of great
lm as can be seen in the Two Mothers. Other note-
orthy 19th century Italian artists are Vincenzo Gemito
ee his beautiful statue of a Fisherboy) who treats his
gures in the manner of the finest Renaissance masters,
d Mosè Bianchi whose "The Washerwomen" confirms
e master as one of the foremost of the literary-artistic
ovement called "Scapigliatura". Medardo Rosso, the
eat Impressionist sculptor, has two rooms to himself.
Iaternity" is one of his best pieces, an intensely

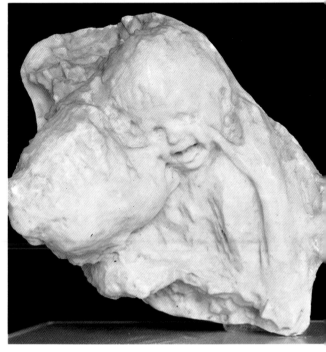

The Gallery of Modern Art - Above: The Dynamism of a Human Body by Umberto Boccioni (left) and Maternity by Medardo Rosso; left: The Anatomy Lesson by Giacomo Favretto; following page: The Washerwomen by Mosè Bianchi.

emotional and poetic treatment of the theme of mothe hood. The Venetian painter Giacomo Favretto is repre sented by several works. The "Anatomy Lesson", is typical example of the painter's ouevre which reveals t influence of his Venetian heritage in the use of delica color and narrative themes. Umberto Boccioni, the gre early 20th century Futurist, is well-represented. H "Dynamism of a Human Body" perfectly illustrates t artist's theory of universal dynamism. Boccioni paints synthesis of what he sees and feels, the objects blendir into one another by the play of light, color, and line. O step beyond Cubism, the object is no longer static an immutable, but dynamic and alive.

The two neo-classical buildings at Porta Venezia.

Porta Venezia seen from above; below: the inside
portico of the Lazzaretto.

PORTA VENEZIA

The two symmetrical Neo-Classical buildings facing eac
other were designed in 1828 by the architect Rodol
Vantini, to form the East Gate, which in 1859 would l
called Porta Venezia to convey the Milanese people
wishes for the speedy liberation of Venice. The doub
gate, opened on three sides by a colonnade, makes a
attractive frame for the bustling Corso Venezia in th
background. This is the place where the Porta Argent
once stood, where Francesco Sforza the new lord of th
city passed, where the Austrians entered the city aft
Napoleon's defeat, where the Milanese valorously foug
their Five Days against the Austrians.

THE LAZZARETTO

The "Lazzaretto" originally a quarantine station, i.e.
special hospital for plague victims, is especially meanin
ful to modernday Italians, for it has an essential role
the classic Italian novel "The Betrothed" which tak
place during the plague epidemic of 1630, although it w
written in the 19th century by the great writer Ale
sandro Manzoni. Now only a wall with six windows is le
of the original rectangular building commissioned l
Ludovico il Moro. Lazzaro Palazzi began work in 148
though, on account of several interruptions, the buildin;
was not finished until 1629. Inside there was a porti
while on the outside were the "isolation wards" for t
plague-stricken, many of whom, incurable, had be
rejected and cast off by all.

Detail of Piermarini's fountain in Piazza Fontana.

PIAZZA FONTANA

The name Piazza Fontana comes from the double pool granite fountain with sea nymphs and dolphins designed Piermarini and put up by Giuseppe Franchi in 1782. From the square right in the heart of downtown Milan, amidst modern buildings, you can glimpse the nearby Cathedral's Gothic pinnacles which create a fascinating contrast – the old mixed with the new, Gothic and contemporary going boldly hand in hand. The square is surrounded by noteworthy buildings such as the Bishop's Palace restored several times by the Borromeos among others, the lovely palace at number 6 with a façade by Piermarini and a magnificent doorway by Pellegrini, and the Palace of the Captain of Justice, once the town courthouse, built in 1586.

The church of Santa Maria della Passione.

SANTA MARIA DELLA PASSIONE

The original plan of the church of Santa Maria della Passione, a Greek cross (equal arms), was designed by Giovanni Battagio between 1482 and 1485, evidently influence, by Bramante. It was later transformed into a Latin cross by Martino Bassi in 1573-1591, who also added the aisles. The church's huge octagonal dome, skillfully decorated with niches and recessing, is typical of all of 16th century Lombard architecture. It w designed by Cristoforo Lombardo who completed it 1530. The Baroque façade, after a design by Giusep Rusnati, is set off by pilasters which probably on served as pedestals for statuary. The interior has ma aged to retain its original Greek cross plan despi Bassi's 16th century transformation.

Detail of the interior of Santa Maria della Passione; below: the porticoed courtyard of the church.

The outside of the former Ospedale Maggiore, also known as Ca' Grande which is currently home of the State University.

OSPEDALE MAGGIORE

Today all that is left of Filarete's plan for his ideal city called *Sforzinda* is the Ospedale Maggiore, now part of the Milan University campus. Filarete devoted himself to the project from 1456 on, when he was awarded the commission by Francesco Sforza and his wife, Bianca Maria Visconti. The original plan called for two separate structures joined by a spacious courtyard. Each structure in turn took in four smaller courtyards marked off by the arms of the transepts, to be used as a men's ward and a women's ward. The building is almost 975 feet long. The part on the right which corresponds to one of the transepts was designed by Filarete who skillfully blended Gothic and Renaissance elements. Above the colonnade portico are double Gothic windows of terracotta, which were created by Guiniforte Solari between 1456 and 1465. 17th century marble busts protrude from the medallions between the arches and at the top of eac[h] upper storey window. The style of the central structu[re] built in the 17th century is, of course, quite differe[nt] although the motifs of the 15th century section ha[ve] been faithfully carried on. The lefthand structure [is] avowedly Neo-Classical, without any decoration at a[ll.] The middle doorway leads us to the huge centr[al] courtyard which was put up in the 17th century, accor[d]ing to the design of Filarete, by Francesco Richini, a[nd] Giovanni Battista Pessina and Fabio Mangone. T[he] double colonnade of slender columns hints at the infl[u]ence of Brunelleschi, the 15th century Florentine arc[hi]tect. The 16th century architects who completed t[he] courtyard are responsible for adding the protrudi[ng] marble busts between the arches which were not i[n]cluded in Filarete's original design.

The façade of San Pietro in Gessate; below: the Synagogue.

SAN PIETRO IN GESSATE

uiniforte Solari was commissioned by the Benedictine
onks to design this church around 1475. It was built
rgely from the donations of two Florentine brothers of
e famous Portinari family (Dante's Beatrice was a
ortinari) whose coat of arms may be seen in the right
ctangular apse. The restoration done on the church in
e 17th century was fortunately eliminated during a
ter restoration in 1910 which brought to light the
urch's typical Lombard façade of single windows
anking a doorway surmounted by round openings. The
terior contains one of the loveliest examples extant of
5th century Milanese painting – the frescoes by Bernar-
no Butinone and Bernardino Zenale depicting scenes
om the life of St. Ambrose, commissioned by Ambrogio
rifi for the Grifi Family Chapel. Set in a mock
rchitecture of pilasters, the frescoes bear the evident
fluence of the Ferrarese school's attention to anatom-
al detail and use of expressionistic color.

SYNAGOGUE

he synagogue with its colored façade was designed in
392 by Luca Beltrami. At Via Guastalla 19 just ahead,
e find the attractive building housing the della Guastal-
 School founded by Countess Torelli di Guastalla to
ovide an education for poverty stricken girls.

The Rotonda della Besana with the church of San Michele at the center; left: interior view of the church's dome.

ROTONDA DELLA BESANA

This unusual area is now a park. Also known as the "Foppone dell'Ospedale" since it once served as burial ground for the Ospedale Maggiore, it was designed by Francesco Raffagno in 1698. The enclosure is composed of a circle of eight big and small segments making an outer arch to which corresponds a portico on the inside. In the center is the church of St. Michael, with a Greek cross plan, designed by Attilio Arrigoni.

The Monument to the Battle of the Five Days by
Giuseppe Grandi; right: detail of the female figures
surrounding the obelisk.

MONUMENT TO THE BATTLE
OF THE FIVE DAYS

The monument is actually a bronze obelisk upon a huge
base decorated with five female figures symbolizing the
"Five Days" from March 18 to 22, 1848. It was designed
by G. Grandi and dedicated in 1895. The crypt contains
the mortal remains of those who perished there, and they
are commemorated every year.

The Idroscalo; below: the ruins of San Giovanni in Conca in Piazza Missori.

IDROSCALO

The idroscalo, built in 1928, is a huge, 7,290 foot long basin spread out over an area of 736,000 square yards. Bleachers for boating fans and boat houses have been put up for the exciting motorboat races held here each year. A corner of the basin has been turned into an attractive little seaside resort the "Riviera di Milano" replete with beach waterfront and all the trappings.

The Velasca Tower.

PIAZZA MISSORI

The square gets its name frome the distinctive equestrian statue dedicated to General Giuseppe Missori designed by Riccardo Ripamonti. The lawn area contains what is left of the apse and crypt of the church of San Giovanni in Conca. The church, probably originally built during the Early Christian period was rebuilt in the 11th century, destroyed by Barbarossa, and once more rebuilt so that the Viscontis could make their family chapel there. Bernabò Visconti was given burial in the church in a tomb decorated with a monument built by the celebrated sculptor Bonino da Campione. In addition, two other interesting buildings look out on the square: the Dei Cavalieri Hotel of 1949 with Emilio Lancia's curved façade and the Superintendency of Education Building adorned with tall columns.

VELASCA TOWER

Towering way above the buildings surrounding it, the Torre Velasca certainly represents an unusual and bold concept of a highrise apartment building. The 345 foot tall skyscraper was designed in 1958 by Ernesto Nathan Rogers, Lodovico Barbiano di Belgioioso and Enrico Peressuti. The tower has stirred up a hornet's nest of controversy: does it or doesn't it clash with the style of the other buildings around it?

SAN NAZARO MAGGIORE

The church was founded by St. Ambrose in 386 who dedicated it to the Holy Apostles and had it erected in the midst of a Christian cemetery. Destroyed by fire in 1075, it was rebuilt in the original Greek cross plan. 19th century tampering altered its stately appearance, though a recent restoration project has brought it back to all its Romanesque glory. The church vestibule contains the celebrated Funerary Chapel of the Trivulzio Family, the only work definitely attributable to Barolomeo Suardi, known as Bramantino, awarded the commission by Gian Giacomo Trivulzio in 1512. The octagonal domed interior, geometrically conceived, is extremely effective. The eight sarcophagi on high bear the remains of members of the Trivulzio family.

Façade and apse of San Nazaro Maggiore; below: **detail of the church's interior and the Trivulzio Chapel.**

The church of Santa Maria in San Satiro.

SAN SATIRO

San Satiro, or more correctly Santa Maria in San Satiro, embodies the architectural concepts of the great architect Donato Bramante. Few traces are left of the original building built by Bishop Ansperto in the 9th century; in 1478 Bramante was commissioned with rebuilding and enlarging the church. Bramante used a single aisle, T-shaped plan, but with an exceptionally large nave and transepts whose grandeur extends right up to the semi-circular dome. Using a clever perspective device, i.e. a painted archway and stucco decoration on the rear wall, Bramante gives the interior the appearance of Greek cross; the presbytery is actually only an optic illusion. A similar spatial feeling is achieved in th adjoining Sacristy, inspired by the Romanesque bapti teries, in which the play of light and form is achieve by the recessing of the niches below and the gallerie above. But each element has another strength and valu The pure lines of the Romanesque baptistery develo into a play of perfectly defined and circumscribe shapes.

SAN SEBASTIANO

San Sebastiano, situated on Via Torino, was commissioned by St. Carlo Borromeo and financed by the city in 1576 in fullfillment of a vow taken with the hope that the terrible plague epidemic would come to an end. The original circular plan was designed by Pellegrini whose design entailed a two storey cylindrical building topped by a dome. Other architects later called in modified the original design and also added a presbytery. The lower level is enhanced by arcades separated by pilaster strips, followed by the cornice with overturned corbels that connect the upper and lower levels with two rows of niches.

The church of San Sebastiano; below: the façade of the church of Sant'Alessandro.

SANT'ALESSANDRO

Amidst droves of Neo-Classical buildings all over Milan, Sant'Alessandro is tucked away in a completely Baroque little corner of the city. The 17th century square is completely dominated by the imposing façade of the church of Sant'Alessandro, one of the loveliest examples of Baroque in Milan. The church, built over the site of a pre-existing medieval building, was designed by a Barnabite monk, Lorenzo Binago, who gave it a round plan with a dome. The rich Baroque façade is accompanied by two belltowers on either side designed by Bianchi in the typical early 18th century style.

Church of Santa Maria presso San Celso, detail of the exterior.

SANTA MARIA PRESSO SAN CELSO

Several artists worked on this building which not unsurprisingly reflects a bit of the undecidedness affecting Lombard art and especially architecture up to the end of the 16th century. The first architect was Giovanni Dolcebuono who designed the T-shaped aisleless plan and the dome. He was succeeded by Solari, Amadeo, Cesariano, Seregni, Alessi, and Bassi. The façade alone would suffice to convey the ferment of the period, undecided as it is between Renaissance simplicity and Baroque flamboyance. Everything is animated, vibrant, overladen with heavy columns, statues, bas-reliefs, statuary inside niches, caryatids, and so forth. Only the octagonal dome peeping out behind the façade is left of Dolcebuono's simple and elegant design.

SAN VINCENZO IN PRATO

eyond the old Naviglio canal city limits stands the tiny
urch of San Vincenzo in Prato, built in the Early
hristian era probably over the site of what was first a
agan burial ground and later a Christian cemetery.
ebuilt by the Benedectine monks, over the centuries its
iginal appearance has been greatly altered. The brick
çade reflects the three part division of the interior into
ave and aisles. The façade is typically Lombard with its
mple design enhanced by little arches and pilaster
rips around the windows. Perhaps the most attractive
art of the façade is the left side with a touch of color
iven by the Roman fragments built into the wall. The
ar is composed of three semi-circular apses, decorated
y pilaster strips, arches, and niches. The calm, light-
led interior has unfortunately been over-restored, but
ill contains several frescoes of great interest.

Left: **Porta Romana in Piazzale Medaglie d'Oro;** right: **the interior of San Vincenzo in Prato;**
top: **exterior view of the church.**

PORTA ROMANA

3uilt in honor of the Austrian princess Marie Margherete
n her way in Madrid to wed Philip II of Spain, the
mpressive gate is located in present-day Piazza Medaglie
'Oro. It is composed of a single huge rusticated stone
rch flanked by piers. The dedicatory inscription which
vas once carved on the architrave has been lost.
Driginally the walls that Gian Maria Olgiati began in

1548 by order of the governor of Milan Ferrante
Gonzaga were to be found nearby. The seven mile, eight
gate walls were built in the shape of a heart with the
Sforzesco Castle set in its hollow. Transformed during
the Napoleonic era, they were gradually torn down until
their complete destruction came about at the end of the
19th century.

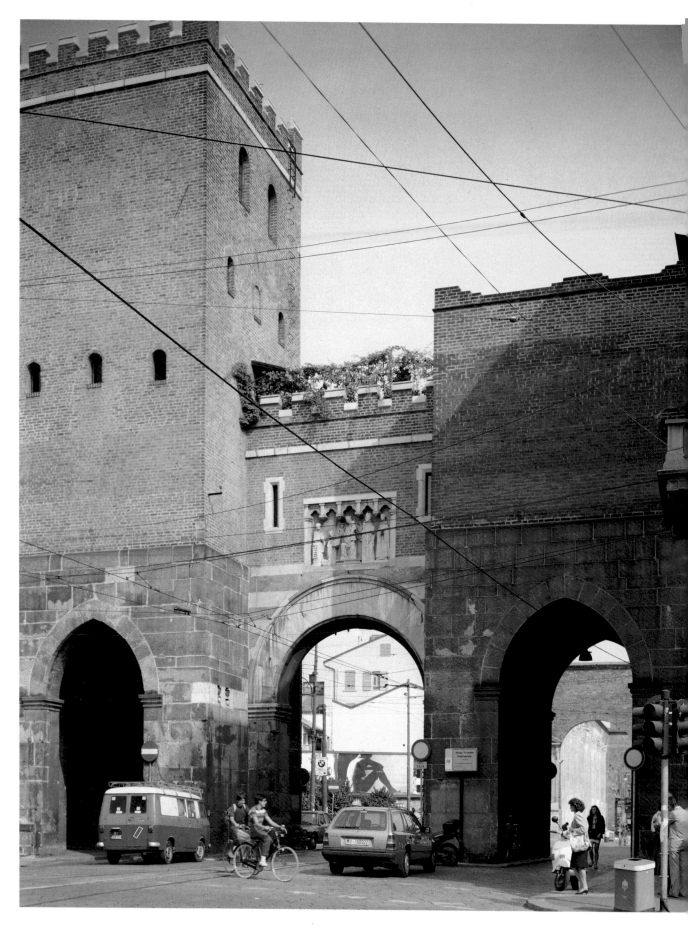

Porta Ticinese dates from the Middle Ages.

Aerial view of the columns and basilica of San Lorenzo Maggiore.

PORTA TICINESE

Porta Ticinese is definitely one of the most unusual remains of the circle of walls put up in 1171 following Barbarossa's destruction of the city and then rebuilt by Azzone Visconti after 1329, although its present appearance is due to a 19th century restoration project. The gate is formed by a great central arch with towers on either side, which in 1861 were opened by two pointed arches. Like every other Milanese gate, Porta Ticinese has been eyewitness to history: after having been assigned to Pavia by Barbarossa in 1162, the gate was scene of the murky events and sly plotting of the Visconti family – Gian Galeazzo Visconti, for example, selected it as the spot to ambush his uncle Bernabò on May 16, 1385.

COLUMNS AND BASILICA OF SAN LORENZO MAGGIORE

In the populous quarter around Porta Ticinese are the most important remains of *Mediolanum*, capital of the Roman Empire of the West: the columns and basilica of San Lorenzo. The juxtaposition of the Roman columns next to the Early Christian basilica creates a truly stirring sight. The sixteen fluted marble columns with Corinthian capitals definitely belonged to a Roman building of the late Imperial period (2nd or 3rd century B.C.), either baths, a temple or a palace. Then, in the 4th century they were brought here and lined up to form the

The basilica of San Lorenzo Maggiore - The Roman columns of the portico.

front of the portico of the Basilica of San Lorenzo, at the time under construction. In the middle of the churchyard is a bronze statue of the emperor Constantine, a copy of the Roman original. The basilica, built between the 4th and 5th centuries, is probably made of material taken from the nearby Roman amphitheater. Its original Early Christian plan was later altered in 1573 by Martino Bassi who managed to preserve much of the original octagonal shape and who is responsible for the dome set on the high drum. Oriental influence has been recognized in the square towers at the four sides with the apses inscribed within the square thus formed; it has been claimed that the plan actually comes from Byzantium. It is fascinating to observe the interior and pick out the Early Christian plan from the 16th century modifications. The chapels of

St. Aquilinus and St. Hippolytus were built adjacent to the basilica in the IV century, while the small mausoleum to St. Sixtus dates from the early 6th century. Destroyed by fires on several occasions, it was rebuilt by Martino Bassi after it collapsed in 1573. Bassi preserved the ancient structure and built the dome over the high drum. The interior is worthy of admiration not only for its sixteenth century style, but also for its early Christian base. Bassi slightly modified the ambulatory which originally ran around the entire central space; he created an octagon between the pillars which create the semi circular structures then comprising the women's gallery above. We can see the same octagonal plan with the women's gallery in the chapel of St. Aquilinus: the central area adorned with niches, women's galleries and

Detail of mosaics in the Chapel of Sant'Aquilino.

The exterior San Lorenzo Maggiore; below: the basilica and surrounding buildings at night.

Interior of the Chapel of Sant'Aquilino: detail.

topped by a dome. The wall paintings extant in San Lorenzo are extremely important, as they are among the few examples of Roman painting left in Milan. In the galleries the motifs created by marble intarsia as wall decoration were repeated in frescoes of the 4th century, though the most beautiful is the mosaic work in the upper hollows of the two end niches, which belong to the late 4th-early 5th century. Judged among the finest examples of Roman mosaics extant in Northern Italy, these, portraying Christ and the Apostles and the Abduction of Elijah, are outstanding for their bright colors and vivacious naturalism. The art of the mosaic had by this time reached a new flowering, although as this mosaic bears witness, those who practiced it never lost sight of the classical canons of order and proportion.

Aerial view of the basilica of Sant'Eustorgio.

SANT'EUSTORGIO

The unassuming façade of a very important church is visible on this pleasant little square. Sant'Eustorgio was commissioned in 515 by Bishop Eustorgio II who had it built over the site of an even older 4th century building put up during the time of Bishop Eustorgio I. At the end of the 11th century the church was rebuilt in the plain Romanesque style and thus it remained until Frederick Barbarossa caused its almost complete destruction in 1164; he even took the Roman sarcophagus supposed to contain the relics of the three Magi to Cologne. In 1190 reconstruction, which would last several centuries, was undertaken: the family chapels on the right side of the church clearly exhibit the various building stages. The 15th century brought the southside chapels and a gem of Renaissance architecture, the Portinari Chapel. The belltower with its typical Lombard decoration of arches and cone-shaped cusp was built between 1297-1309. The single aisle church with a 225 foot long nave conveys a sense of vastness, increased by the optical illusion deriving from a slight inclination of the massive piers going down the nave. The church contains so many ar treasures it might well be called a museum. The Brivi Chapel, recently restored to its Renaissance splendo with the tombs of Giacomo Stefano Brivio by th brothers Francesco and Tommaso Cazzaniga and Briosc and the Torelli Chapel with the Gothic arch on twiste columns used as Pietro Torelli's sepulchre, are tw noteworthy examples. The Visconti Chapel contains th tomb of Stefano Visconti, a Gothic masterpiece b Giovanni di Balduccio. The frescoes decorating th chapel bear Tuscan influence, namely that of Giotto. Th marble altar frontal with scenes of the Passion of Chris left unfinished, is a masterpiece, though it was worke on throughout many periods by many great but anony mous sculptors among which we may pick out In ternational style, (perhaps even Giovannino de' Grass Campionese, and Florentine masters. Finally we come t the pure Renaissance Portinari Chapel commissioned b the Florentine Pigello Portinari in 1462 and finished i 1468, the year of his death. The chapel is a blend of th

The basilica of Sant'Eustorgio; below: the large, central nave of the basilica.

115

Sant'Eustorgio - The Slaughter of the Innocents by Cristoforo Storer; below: Crucifix, early 14th century and 'Madonna del Latte', 15th century Lombard painter.

116

Sant'Eustorgio - Madonna and Child with St. James and St. Augustine by Bergognone; below:
The Martyrdom of St. Peter the Martyr by Cristoforo Bossi.

Details of the interior of the dome of the Portinari Chapel and one of the frescoes by Vincenzo Foppa that adorn the chapel walls; opposite page: the tomb of St. Peter the Martyr, the masterpiece by Giovanni di Balduccio at the center of the Portinari Chapel.

finest Tuscan architecture with the painting of Vincenzo Foppa, a new star in the late 15th century Lombard firmament. The frescoes high up on the walls, were discovered in 1878 and restored at the beginning of the 20th century. They are truly Foppa's great masterpiece. At first the architect was actually believed to be the Florentine Michelozzo, but today it is felt that the church was designed by a Lombard master under Tuscan influence. The outside is square shape with four corner structures and surmounted by a dome enhanced by tondos. The interior, also square, is decorated with Foppa's stucco angels. In the center of the chapel stands the famous Tomb of St. Peter Martyr, built by Giovanni di Balduccio, a follower of the great Pisan Innovator,

Giovanni Pisano, between 1336 to 1339. Giovanni d Balduccio's work is a milestone in Lombard sculpture' march towards the Renaissance, a harmonious blendin; of the classical Renaissance and sinuous vibrant Gothi line. The tomb, which in 1734 was moved from the lef nave of the Basilica to the Portinari Chapel consists o an elaborate white marble urn supported by eigh statues of Virtues resting on them. The bas-relie decorations on the urn depict scenes from the life of St Peter Martyr. A tricuspidate niche above the lid of th sarcophagus contains statues of the Virgin and Chil between Sts. Dominic and Peter Martyr, statues o Christ giving His Blessing and two angels stand abov the niche.

Porta Ticinese, a neo-classical design by Luigi Cagnola.

PORTA TICINESE

The purest Milanese Neo-Classic is exemplified in this work by Luigi Cagnola who erected it between 1801 and 1814. It was financed by public donations to celebrate Napoleon's victory at Marengo. Built of Baveno granite, it is composed of an entablature resting on eight Ionic columns. In 1815 when the Napoleonic storm had died down in Europe, the arch was dedicated to peace.

NAVIGLIO GRANDE

The Naviglio Grande belongs to the network of water ways that from the Middle Ages on sparked the develop ment of agriculture in the countryside surrounding the city and, at the same time, constituted one of the city's main traffic thoroughfares. Navigable from the 13th century, they were a well-known characteristic of Mila nese life, until the postwar period when most of them were covered to comply with the new town planning laws. Around the canal are typical Milanese apartment buildings, with their long inner balconies, rising amidst intricate webs of small picturesque streets.

Views of the Naviglio.

Examples of Art Nouveau architecture in Milan.

ART NOUVEAU HOUSES

Even though art nouveau did not take root in Italy as in other European countries, still we can find interesting examples of this style in Milan. The new artistic movement spread from Turin and found its most fertile terrain in Milan, especially with Giuseppe Sommaruga whose Castiglioni Palace of 1903 is the highpoint of Lombard art nouveau. His houses on Via Bellini and Via Spadari whose balconies are decorated with flower motifs and unusual sculptural designs that confer strong emphasis and vigorous expressiveness to the building. The artist's imagination is unleashed especially in the wrought iron balconies on the outside and gates on the street, giving the façade a refined and elegant look.

The Home for Elderly Musicians in Piazza Buonarroti with Enrico Butti's monumento to
Giuseppe Verdi, 1918.

Above left: **Palazzo Belgioioso**; above: **Via Morone**;
below: **the home of Alessandro Manzoni.**

VIEWS OF MILAN

he Home for Elderly Musicians, erected in the Venetian
yle in 1899 and enlarged after the Second World War,
a foundation set up by Giuseppe Verdi to shelter
derly impoverished musicians. The crypt contains the
ortal remains of Verdi and his second wife. In the
urtyard is a monument to Arrigo Boito by Secchi
)23).

e Palazzo Belgioioso, a 19th century work by Piermari-
, dominates the square of the same name. The façade,
teworthy for its elegance, sports a rusticated stone
se enhanced by semicolums surmounted by a triangu-
r pediment.

a Morone nr. 1 (photo above right) is the entrance to
e Home of Alessandro Manzoni, one of Italy's greatest
th century writers who lived here from 1814 until his
ath (May 22, 1873). Today restored, the brick building
uses the National Manzoni Society and the Manzoni
useum.

Interior and exterior views of San Siro Stadium
dedicated to Giuseppe Meazza.

SAN SIRO

The San Siro Municipal Stadium, named after tl
famous soccer champion Giuseppe Meazza, was built
1926 to serve as the home field for the "Milan" team.
was enlarged during the fifties, and then revamped ar
expanded for the 1990 World Cup Games. Other spo
facilities in the San Siro district include two rac
courses, the Ippodromo and the Trottatoio, for point-t
point and steeple-chasing, and trotting, respectivel
Both race courses were built in the early twenties.

The Abbey of Chiaravalle, Cistercian monastery founded in the 12th century, near Milan.

BBEY OF CHIARAVALLE

the immediate surroundings of Milan is one of the first
d most important Cistercian abbeys, founded in 1135
St. Bernard, abbot of Clairvaux (in Italian: Chiaraval-
. Here in this area once called Rovegnano, the
stercian monks created one of their most vital centers
om both a religious and an artistic standpoint. After
ving drained what was then marshland, they built a
lendid architectural complex on the spot, of which only
e church is still standing today. Looking at it from afar
makes a splendid impression with its simple form,
urdy buttresses, and drum, out of which rises the
aring 14th century tower, with its lively contrast of
ite arches against red brick. The church is a blend of

the French Gothic and Lombard Romanesque traditions:
the use of buttresses and Gothic arches, elements clearly
inspired by French architecture are joined with local
motifs such as the arch decoration on the façade, sides,
and ends of the transepts. The plan retains its T-shape
form with cylindrical piers dividing the nave from the
aisles and, for the first time in Italy, pointed arches
delineated by subtle ribbing. Last but not least, the
influence of Tuscan Art – the Sienese School and perhaps
even the Giottesque Florentine School – was keenly felt
by the unknown masters who frescoed scenes from the
life of the Virgin upone the walls of the octagonal dome
during the early 14th century.

LEGEND

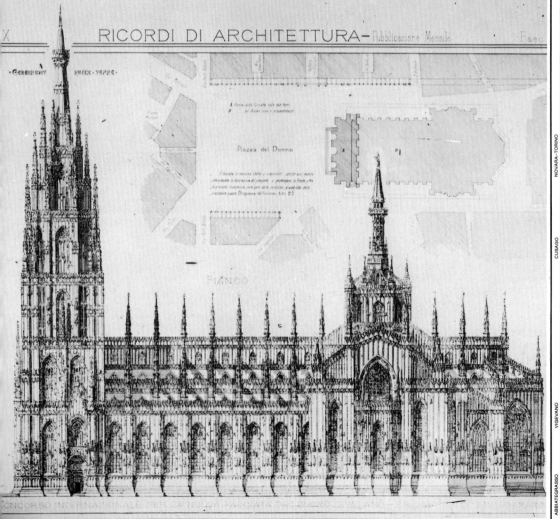

RICORDI DI ARCHITETTURA- Pubblicazione Mensile

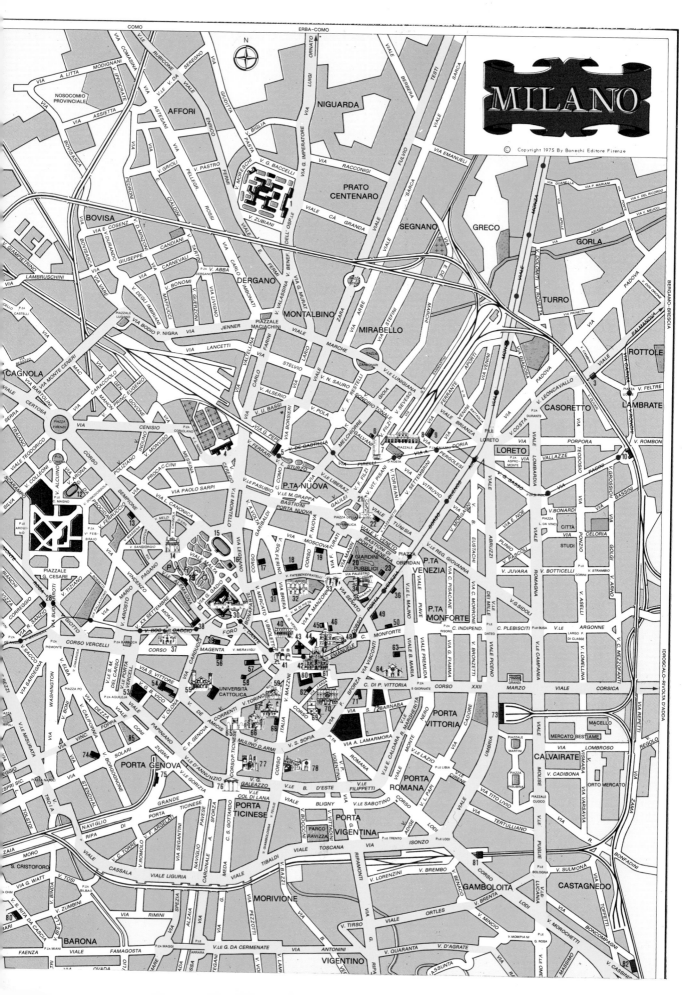

INDEX

Lire 12.000

ISBN 88-7204-011-